Death Is a Noun

Death Is a Noun/
A View of the End of Life

by John Langone

Little, Brown and Company/
Boston/Toronto

FOURTH PRINTING
T 09/72

The lines from "Do not go gentle into that good night" by Dylan Thomas are reprinted by permission of New Directions Publishing Corporation from *The Poems of Dylan Thomas*, copyright 1952 by Dylan Thomas.

```
Library of Congress Cataloging in Publication Data

Langone, John, 1929-
   Death is a noun.

   SUMMARY: Discusses the biological meaning of death,
attitudes of the dying, survivors, and society toward it,
and such related topics as euthanasia, abortion, murder,
suicide, and immortality.
   1. Death--Juvenile literature.  [1.  Death]
I.  Title.
BD444.L375          128'.5          70-189261
ISBN 0-316-514209
```

Published simultaneously in Canada
by Little, Brown & Company (Canada) Limited

PRINTED IN THE UNITED STATES OF AMERICA

For my father, Joseph,
who died before I could know him.
For my mother, who read to me—
and for Dolores,
who understands me.

Contents

One

Death's Mystery

Death comes to everything that lives. Of that we can be sure. Men and mice, birch trees and bacteria — all must die one day. Death is a part of life, and one cannot be without the other. It is the other side of the coin, the other bank of the river, the only medicine for the fatal illness we know as life. It is a necessary end, as Shakespeare said, that "will come when it will come." It is, in the words of Edna St. Vincent Millay, "the keen mind suddenly gone deaf and blind." It is the sentence that hangs over man's head from the moment he is born. And it is, some believe, the debt a sinful mankind owes to the Creator of all life.

Death may be an unwelcome, terrifying enemy, a skeleton with an evil grin who clutches an ugly scythe in his bony hand. Or death may be a long-awaited friend who waits quietly, invisibly, beside the bed of a dying patient to ease his pain, his loneliness, his weariness, his hopelessness.

Man alone among the things that live knows that death will come. Mice and trees and microbes do not. And man, knowing that he has to die, fears death, the great unknown, as a child fears the dark. "We fear to be we know not what, we know not where," said John Dryden. But what man dreads more is the dying, the relentless process in which he passes into extinction, alone and helpless and despairing. So he puts death and dying out of his mind, denying that they exist, refusing to discuss them openly, trying desperately to control them. He coins phrases like "Never say die," and somehow, when he says something is "good for life," he means forever. Unable to bear the thought of ceasing to be, he comforts himself with thoughts of a pleasant afterlife in which he is rewarded for his trials on earth, or he builds monuments to himself to perpetuate at least his memory if not his body.

Man did not always deny death as he does now. In medieval times, death was everywhere. War, famine and plague cast their dark shadow across the land, and man lived in a state of constant dread. Heaven, it seemed, was ignored, and always the emphasis was on the horrors of hell and death, on the gruesome, on rotting corpses and menacing devils. The Dance of Death theme — cavorting demons and skeletons leading men, women and children to the infernal regions — appeared frequently in the art of the age, and later in the works of such masters as Hieronymus Bosch, Albrecht Dürer and Hans Holbein. Its message was always the same: death is the equalizer, and man must never forget it.

Gradually, however, with progress in medical science, man has begun to think more about warding off the grim reaper and less about death and dying. The emphasis is on healing, on a better and longer life. Transplants and wonder drugs are in; death is out, unpopular and unsung.

Nevertheless, death remains with us. Men die of natural causes, of sickness and accidents, by their own hand or by that of others. So it is better to face it, in a sensible way, as fearlessly as possible, than to deny it, for there is more to it than simply dust returning to earth.

There are things to be learned about death and dying that have been overlooked amid the fear and the mystery, and it is these things that some scientists, theologians and lawyers are now beginning to investigate and discuss more objectively and openly.

For example, we must reevaluate our thinking about when the life of a human being really ends. It is not when breathing stops, because the sophisticated gadgetry of medicine can restore that breathing for long periods of time. It is not when the heart stops beating, for that, too, may be started up again mechanically — or it may be removed and transplanted into the chest of another, there to pick up its beat of life again.

There are the moral questions involved in deciding who shall live and who shall die. Who receives the organ graft? When does a doctor turn off the life-sustaining equipment? Is it ever right to deliberately end the life of a dying, suffering, incurable patient? Is it right for a doctor to keep a patient alive if he will be little more than a vegetable? The issue of abortion also raises important questions. Is the fetus a human being? Is abortion murder? When, actually, does life begin?

There is capital punishment, also fraught with controversy. Does the Biblical "eye for an eye" justify legal execution? Does putting a murderer to death really prevent crime, as some believe? Murder raises many questions, too. Why do people kill? Is it some brain defect that pulls the trigger, or is it an environment of poverty or something in the killer's childhood? Similar questions can be asked about suicide.

There are questions dealing with what patients think when the moment of their death nears, or when they are first told they will die. Do people face death calmly, angrily, fearfully? What can we learn from the dying patient that will help the living?

There is the matter of prolongation of life. Will man ever achieve the ancient dream of immortality? Will he lengthen his life-span?

And finally, is death the end of everything? What happens after we die? Does the soul live on in some other body or some other place?

These are some of the difficult questions which will be discussed in the pages that follow. There are no single, simple answers — questions involving ethics, morality, medical research, the law and religion seldom are answered easily, and to everyone's satisfaction. About all one can do is examine each point of view carefully, recognize that there is disagreement and then make a personal judgment. But first, one must be willing to approach the subjects of death and dying in a way that removes them from the grave, as one would approach any topic of study. Death is a noun, and it and dying are very much a part of the story of life. It behooves us to read the story in its entirety.

Two

When Is a
Person Dead?

Out, out are the lights, out all.
And over each quivering form,
The curtain, a funeral pall,
Comes down with the rush of a storm.

Edgar Allan Poe's interpretation of death, although it might satisfy men of letters, obviously would be of no help to a team of surgeons about to remove a man's heart so that it might be placed in another human being. Neither, however, would the medical profession's own long-held definition of death as "the apparent extinction of life, manifested by the absence of heartbeat and respiration." Granted, this is better than the standard dictionary definition of death as simply "the end of life" or the poet's "chain of consciousness snapped asunder." But not much. For these are not definitions at all in this age of the transplant and what medical science calls spare-part surgery.

Men of science now know that our bodily organs and tissues die at different rates, and that a stilled heart can be revived, made to beat again, with massage, stimulants and electric shock. Moreover, it is possible to keep both heart and lungs functioning, the patient "alive," with such equipment as respirators, which force air into the lungs, and heart-lung machines that pump the blood

9

and enrich it with oxygen, allowing surgeons to work on a dry, bypassed heart.

Nor can the lack of function of what we know as the mind be taken alone as proof of death, for some unconscious persons live on while breathing without mechanical assistance. In fact, some thirty disorders can cause a deathlike trance, including asphyxiation, catalepsy, epilepsy, cerebral anemia, apoplexy, smallpox, cholera, shock, influenza, freezing and being struck by lightning. At Cornell Medical Center a few years ago, doctors studied fourteen patients who were, for all intents and purposes, clinically dead, and yet recovered under special treatment. There also was the celebrated case of the brilliant Soviet physicist Lev Landau, who was brought four times out of a state of clinical death following an automobile accident.

Given all of this, it becomes apparent that the legal criterion of death — a declaration by a licensed physician that he has been unable to record any pulse, heartbeat and respiration — must be reworked so that it may be plugged into the now generation of medicine. For should a surgeon remove a patient's heart or other vital organ before an acceptable declaration of death has been issued, or should he fail to use supportive measures at the proper time, he could be left open to criminal action.

No more can we be guided by King Lear's analysis of Cordelia's state: "She's gone forever! I know when one is dead, and when one lives. She's dead as earth. Lend me a looking-glass. If that her breath will mist or stain the stone, why, then she lives."

A recent case in Great Britain illustrates the difficulty. A man who suffered a skull fracture was operated on for removal of a blood clot from the surface of his brain. At 11 A.M. on a Sunday, twenty-four hours after the fracture was received, the man quit breathing and had to be helped along by a respirator. Later, the man's wife was asked to permit surgeons to remove one of his kidneys for grafting into the body of another man whose previous graft had failed. The woman agreed, believing that the kidney would be removed after death. At 11 A.M. on Monday, the unconscious man — with heart beating, kidneys working and breathing maintained artificially — was taken to the operating room where the surgeons removed his kidney and transplanted it. The respirator was stopped after the operation, and the body was taken to the morgue. The surgeon was charged with manslaughter. At a hearing, he insisted that death had actually occurred when respiration stopped at 11 A.M. on Sunday, and a pathologist testified that death had been inevitable. (Also raised was the question of whether the person who stopped the respirator was guilty of homicide, a point which will be discussed in a subsequent chapter.) One opinion in the case (eventually dismissed) was that there could be no distinction between medical and legal death, and that the decision must rest with the doctor.

In another case, in Houston, the heart of a thirty-six-year-old man who had died as the result of a beating received in a brawl was transplanted into a sixty-two-year-old man. A county medical examiner speculated at the time that when the donor's assailants went to trial, the defense might contend that the donor died because his heart was removed for the graft. In at least two cases since 1968, where the donor was the victim of murder, defense attorneys did contend that the surgeons caused death by removing the heart. Lawyers, however, have expressed doubt that this point will affect the outcome of trials in such cases.

It is easy to understand why the heart has played a key role in the cases cited here, and in any discussion of life and death. It is the body's workhorse, beating seventy times a minute; each time it "makes a muscle" it pushes out a half-cup of blood. In fifty years of relentless labor, the heart muscle pumps three hundred thousands tons — with a total expenditure of energy large enough to haul a ship out of water. Caricatured on Valentine cards, won and broken and left in San Francisco, the heart symbolizes love, the courage of kings and lions, and physical strength. Clinical studies of patients undergoing open-heart surgery reveal that the patients view operations of this kind as a realistic threat to life, and surgeons have coined the expression "cardiac psychosis" for the reaction.

Today, the trend among those concerned with finding new definitions of death — physicians, lawyers, theologians — is toward the absence of brain activity rather than cessation of heartbeat and respiration. "Despite a recordable heartbeat and audible respiration," remarked

When Is a Person Dead?

Dr. Hannibal Hamlin of the Department of Neurosurgery of Massachusetts General Hospital, "the person dies when the beat of the brain has become irretrievable. The human personality lives in the brain, not the heart."

If death does come when the brain's beat quits forever, as Dr. Hamlin says, how does the physician determine this? What tools does he use to pronounce a person dead, now that he can no longer rely simply on the ceasing of heartbeat and breathing? The answer lies in a tracing of the brain's electrical activity called an electroencephalogram (EEG), or brain-wave pattern.

Electroencephalography is based on the fact that the live brain generates very small electrical currents, even during sleep or deep coma. It is said that each person has a brain-wave pattern as distinctive as his handwriting. These waves — the result of changes in the brain current — may appear at a frequency of ten per second, but vary in frequency and size. These currents are recorded by attaching tiny wires called electrodes to the scalp, and connecting them to a vacuum-tube amplifier. There they are magnified some one million times, and made to activate an electromagnetic pen that writes the EEG as an ink line on a moving strip of paper. When the brain wave expresses itself as a flat line on the EEG paper, then the brain cells are dead, and so, too, is the patient, legally and medically. (This, however, may be disputed in some cases, as we shall see later on.)

Man can live for weeks without food, and for a few days without water; but deprived of oxygen, his skeletal muscles will not contract, his heart will not beat, and his brain cells fail. The heart, as we have noted, can be revived and assisted. But with the brain, it is not so easy.

Physicians who adhere to the brain-death test feel that with the brain in a flat-wave state and unresponsive to outside stimuli such as a flashing light, little is gained by keeping the human body technically alive by artificial means. There is no point, they maintain, in allowing the blood to circulate and the lungs to breathe if the patient is doomed to live out a vegetable existence if he survives. The brain is not always irreversibly damaged when the heart stops, and with the EEG the doctor can determine how much permanent damage has occurred. (For instance, a drowning victim may show a pattern corresponding to a state of "functional arrest," meaning that the damage is at least partly reversible.) A patient cannot, however, be maintained indefinitely on a respirator, even though the heart continues to beat. With brain death, tremendous pressure builds up inside the skull, and the body develops what is known medically as diabetes insipidus. Large amounts of urine are lost, and without massive infusions of fluid, blood vessels will collapse. The result is heart stoppage, despite the fact that the lungs are functioning with the aid of a respirator. A human system supported too long opens the way to lung infection, and even though the heart may be started up again, it will finally cease permanently. (Thus far, the longest anyone has been kept alive with a machine is six and a half days.)

When Is a Person Dead?

In all fifty states, the question of human death is treated as a question of fact to be decided in every case. When doubt arises, the court will ask medical experts to testify about the time of death, on the assumption that physicians agree. This, however, is not the case, for the means of determining death are still not hard and fast, and physicians often disagree. In a recent heart-transplant case, two physicians had differing opinions over a ruling that the donor was legally dead while his heart continued to beat for several hours. One of the doctors pronounced the donor dead at 11:30 A.M., more than three hours before the transplant operation, because of the absence of brain waves. The other, however, said at 2 P.M. that he thought the man might still be alive. A conference was held, and it was decided to accept the first doctor's ruling.

The brain-wave test itself, as we have suggested earlier, may be disputed in some cases. In the medical literature are a number of cases of persons still alive after temporary disappearance of their brain waves. At a meeting of leading brain surgeons in Israel in 1968, it was reported that five patients at a medical center recovered from serious injuries after lying inert for weeks, during which time their brain waves were undetectable. One of them, a fifteen-year-old boy who had fallen into a pit, had no spontaneous breathing and no evidence of brain activity for two weeks. Another, a boy of fourteen wounded in the head during the Six-Day War, recovered after a three-week coma, which included a period when he had no brain waves. The doctors said he subsequently returned to normal, physically and mentally. The same year, a Tokyo physician announced that in the past ten years he had treated fifteen patients, including infants, who had lived for a considerable time after their brain waves had disappeared. One of the patients was an infant who continued to breathe naturally for ten days after the brain waves disappeared. Of the fifteen, five recovered their brain waves completely; the others lived from forty minutes to ten days.

Laboratory experiments also have added evidence disputing the long-held opinion that the brain dies for good once it is deprived of blood-borne oxygen. Scientists, for instance, have demonstrated that an isolated cat's brain can be kept frozen for more than two hundred days, and then brought "back to life" by circulating warm blood through it. In this particular experiment, when the brain was brought out of its deep freeze and checked with an EEG, the brain-wave pattern that resulted was identical to that of a live cat. Brain nerve cells, which sop up oxygen at a high rate, die within three to six minutes after the blood flow is stopped. But in the cat study, what the scientists were able to show was that the brain can be kept in a state of preservation, a resting state, so to speak. Research also has demonstrated that animals can be kept alive without a brain or nervous system. Dr. Robert J. White, a Cleveland neurosurgeon noted for his work on isolating the living brain, has succeeded in maintaining dogs and monkeys for up to four hours after EEG death with mechanical and chemical assistance. Such a technique might be helpful in preserving cadaver organs for transplants.

The very fact that an isolated brain kept up its electrical activity *in vitro* — the scientists' way of describing experiments that are carried out in the laboratory — is rather startling, and does lend some support to those who feel it may be necessary to continue artificial respiration in medical treatment of a human being even after the brain waves stop functioning. Some view such experiments, and the cases of patients who have recovered after showing flat brain waves, as evidence that patients can survive seemingly hopeless injuries, even though some may be incapacitated; doctors, then, would have to think twice before switching off life-sustaining machinery.

Many scientists, while conceding that life does, in fact, reside in the brain, feel that brain waves cannot be measured sufficiently accurately with present techniques. (In some hospital settings, the brain-wave meter cannot even be installed because of electrical interference by such sources as fluorescent light.) There also is the critical question of how many hours should pass after cessation of brain waves before it can be decided that death has actually taken place. Some believe that physicians should be required to use as a guide the clinical case in which life was maintained for the longest period of time after the brain waves stopped. Thus a surgeon could not immediately carry out a heart transplant if there was on record, say, a case of a donor who had lived for four weeks after his brain waves stopped.

He would have to wait the four weeks. (By that time, however, a transplanter might argue, the heart would be worthless as a graft.) This means that enormous faith must be placed in the brain-wave meter, and many doctors are asking whether it can be trusted to such an extent. On the other hand, numerous practitioners believe that instrument fault might make it possible to miss the exact moment of irreversible brain damage of a person already dead, but that it is impossible to mistakenly declare a living person dead.

It is obvious, then, that to determine the moment of death — or the moment at which brain damage reaches the point of no return — is no easy matter. Up to now, we have been discussing death of the brain and death of the heart. These refer to parts of the body. But when one traces the death of one of these parts inward, what is arrived at is the death of cells, without which there can be no life. Every second, some fifty million of our body's cells die, replaced in the same period of time by an equal number. Some cells live longer than others: red blood cells last about a hundred and twenty days, white cells about thirteen; nerve cells can live a hundred years. Thus, the whole business of determining death may end up being one of chemistry, and some scientists suggest that if something stronger than a doctor's opinion should resolve the question of death, it may be biochemical testing.

Since death is a gradual process at the cellular level, with tissues differing in their ability to live without oxygen, it is clear that the point of death of various cells and organs is not as important as the surety that what has occurred is irreversible — that the patient is truly gone. And the determination of this, in the judgment of most physicians today, has to be based on the clinical knowledge of a doctor supplemented by a number of diagnostic aids, of which the EEG is currently the most useful.

One of the first and most acceptable definitions of brain death was set forth in 1968 by the Ad Hoc Committee of the Harvard Medical School under the title "A Definition of Irreversible Coma." An organ, brain, or other part that no longer functions, the committee said, and has no possibility of functioning again, is for all practical purposes dead.

How does one go about diagnosing a permanently nonfunctioning brain, and thereby the death of an individual?

Applying the committee's guidelines, let us examine a patient who appears to be in a deep coma. The following picture of irreversible coma — death — emerges. The patient is unreceptive and unresponsive; that is, he does not react even to pain: he does not groan or wince, and there is no quickening of his breathing. There is no muscular movement and no spontaneous breathing for at least an hour, or for three minutes if a mechanical respirator is shut down. He has no reflexes, does not move his eyes, and does not blink. The EEG printout is flat. And when all of these tests are repeated twenty-four hours later, there is no change. (The validity of these data as indications of irreversible cerebral damage, the committee added, depends on the exclusion of two conditions: hypothermia, in which body temperature is below 90 degrees, or central nervous system depression due to drugs such as barbiturates.)

It can hardly be questioned, then, that death is the permanent cessation of *all* the body's key functions; no single factor, such as stoppage of respiration or heart action or nervous system activity, can be considered sufficient by itself to establish a diagnosis of death. Dr. Vincent J. Collins of the Northwestern University School of Medicine has suggested monitoring five areas — heart, brain, lungs, circulation and reflex action — every fifteen minutes over a period of one to two hours before pronouncing a person dead. Each of the areas would be scored 2, 1, or 0, according to whether the function was going on, depressed or stopped. A total score of 5 or more would indicate potential life, even if the patient appeared dead.

With respect to the question of how long the brain must be stopped before death can be attested to, some specialists say there is enough evidence to indicate that survival in the face of various clinical signs and a flat EEG for even one hour is impossible. They maintain, therefore, that a patient should be considered dead if the signs are present continuously for two hours, and argue that the twenty-four-hour wait in the Harvard guidelines might be too long, particularly in cases where the heart is to be transplanted. With regard to survivals on record after EEG stoppage, it has been pointed out that most reports of flat EEG's with eventual recovery were found, on close examination, to be not really without electrical activity. (According to some pathologists, the longest period of electrically neutral recording with eventual recovery is about one hundred and twenty minutes.)

Regardless of whether we change the medicolegal concept of death from death of the heart to death of the brain, one basic question has to be considered: What, exactly, is death? In trying to answer this question in its broadest sense, we face the idea that the end of a human being's life-span cannot be discussed without considering what we know as the spirit, the *anima*, the soul. Often, a person kept alive in a hospital by tubes, blood, fluids and machinery is merely a body and not, even in the view of some theologians, a being. The Reverend Paul McCleave, a Presbyterian clergyman and director of the Department of Medicine and Religion of the American Medical Association, has suggested that the time has come to recognize that there are three types of death: organic death, cellular death, and death of the being, or spiritual death.

"Long after I have been pronounced physiologically dead and the mortician has set me in the ground," he says, "I remind you that cellularly I am still alive. My fingernails grow, my hair grows for three to six weeks, and it is a long time before I return to dust. As a clergyman, I believe that the physiological determination of death should be left to the physician, whose knowledge and experience qualify him to make that decision. However, there is another area that needs to be considered

— the interpretation of meaningful life, life beyond the mere presence of physical processes. I believe that spiritual death takes place when someone no longer can function as a meaningful person. In other words, he no longer can be responsive to others or to the world around him; therefore, he no longer is a being."

Three

Facing Death

When death approaches, people face it in different ways. They may go to meet it calmly, as do the aged, the incurable and the unwanted in a place called Sago Lane in Singapore's Chinatown. Lying on oilcloth-covered wooden pallets placed side by side in "death houses," there the dying wait — for days, weeks or years — for death to carry them to a world of comfort and peace. There is no entertainment, no laughter, no conversation as they await their grim visitor. Others meet death by turning to religion, preparing themselves spiritually to accept their fate as God's will; some individuals, told they have but a few weeks left, begin indulging themselves in food, drink and one entertainment after another; still others pursue a more intellectual course — reading, writing, learning.

Death can be welcomed as a release from pain, cursed as a hideous thing that has cut short a productive and happy life, fought as it beckons a condemned man up the steps to the gallows or down the corridor to the gas chamber. Death is denied by those who, refusing to accept that their days are numbered, cling stubbornly to life, seek new cures and treatments, and grasp at any straw of hope. And when death threatens or takes someone dear to us, we react with painful grief, disbelief, anger, shock.

Facing Death

Antoine de Saint-Exupéry, a French novelist and aviator, has recorded his reflections in the face of death. In *Flight to Arras*, an autobiographical account of a perilous wartime mission, he wrote that he had never known of a man to think of himself when dying. In the instant one is about to give up his body, he learns to his amazement how little store he sets by that body: "It is in your act that you exist, not in your body. Your act is yourself, and there is no other you. Your body belongs to you: it is not you." He went on to say that man imagines that it is death he fears; but what he fears is the unforeseen, the "explosion."

Tales of the supernatural emphasize the horror and the mystery of death. We read of coffins and candles and draperies of black, and we hear muffled drums, the creaking gates of cemeteries and the banshees' wail. Even religious teaching, although it is a source of great comfort to many of the dying, might be blamed for much of the dread associated with death — such as the words of the Mass of the Dead that tell us of "sharp flames," "the bottomless pit," "the torments of hell," "the day of wrath," and "the mouth of the lion." But it probably is true that man fears dying more than death. The known is not as fearsome and terrifying as the unknown. Man also has a tendency to fear the physical pain that is supposed to accompany the end of life. We have been conditioned to feel that way. There are expressions like "last gasp," "death rattle" and "death throes." In the newspapers, we read of mountain climbers crushed in a rock fall, linemen electrocuted on a high-wire job, miners asphyxiated in an underground prison, swimmers drowned, babies smothered in their cribs, and various people shot, stabbed, poisoned, kicked and clubbed to death.

All of these things make us put dying in the same category with all that is dreadful and physically painful. We ask ourselves, "Will it hurt?" So preoccupied are we with our physical selves that we see everything — even the spirit world — in the same physical sense: flames in hell, golden thrones in heaven, choirs of angels, ghosts in sheets, an iron pitchfork in the hand of Satan.

[We don't really know death, so we fear it, but the closer one is to a death he has contemplated for some time the less that particular death is likely to be feared.] Were one to let a black widow spider loose in the Death Row cell of a condemned murderer, chances are he'd panic. The fact that the condemned man is on his way to execution does not make him unafraid of the spider. The convict, while he might fear the spider, has lived so long with the thought of his death at the hands of the state that he can be indifferent to it at the same time. Men who live in the very shadow of death — on a battlefield or in a life-threatening job — do not fear it nearly so much as do those who have never been close to war or have never gone beneath the ground with a mining crew.

You can also be reassured that it probably is worse to be uncertain about *whether* one will die at a particular moment than to actually die. This is so because dying people, in most cases, are numbed by pain-killing or tranquilizing medicines or by the ailment itself, which can weaken them to such an extent that awareness ebbs to haziness. From this semisleep, the dying gradually pass into death, or what may be called permanent sleep by those who believe that all ends there. The transition usually is an easy one. If the analogy with sleep is true — and it has been said that sleep is but temporary death — then the act of dying is not the terror-filled trip that moviemakers and short-story writers make it out to be. None of us is aware of the exact moment we pass from waking to sleeping. It is doubtful that any of us will be aware of that moment when we pass from being to ceasing to be, when we melt softly away, like a snow-flake. Even in cases of sudden death, it is unlikely that there is any sudden burst of awareness that all is over, or any great flash of pain. The time element has to be present for any physical sensation to be felt, and in sudden death that element is lacking. If there were any awareness or pain in sudden death, it probably would be too momentary to be recorded. In 1935, the head of a large sanitarium in Norway reported that death is a pleasant experience, accompanied by an intense feeling of bodily well-being and happiness. He had tried to detect how human beings feel when death is very close. Even though the patient appeared to be in great pain, in every case, the doctor said, he had the impression that death was associated with contentment.

A great deal of attention is being paid nowadays to studying the dying and the effects of their situation on the living. Scientists are trying to find out what dying patients think about when death nears, whether they are afraid or bitter or blissful. For years, the terminally ill were neglected from a research standpoint. There were several reasons for this. One was a feeling among researchers that it was not right to do what might seem heartless probing at such a time of crisis. Another was the attitude that since death was inevitable, little could be gained by studying the dying. Medical people, also, generally avoid the subject of death, if for no other reason than it is the negation of what they are dedicated to — preserving life. Too much discussion and concern over death tends to focus on their inability to guarantee long life. And so death is treated in a businesslike way. A person is sick, or injured in an accident, or assaulted, or harms himself. An attempt is made to save his life. Except for a few words of comfort, a reassuring smile and a pat on the cheek, nothing else is said or done. The patient dies. The relatives grieve. The doctors and the nurses concern themselves with another patient. There is a funeral, and a burial and a few prayers. We are born, we die. That's life, and nothing will alter the script.

But as scientists have begun to change their minds about studying the dying, it has become evident that there is much of value to be learned. For instance, it is now apparent that when physicians, nurses, family or friends refuse to talk about death to people who are dying, the feelings of helplessness and isolation that gnaw at the dying patient are magnified. These feelings, in many cases, are harder to bear than the threat of death itself. Many patients know they are dying anyway, and if those in attendance persist in saying, "Everything is going to be fine," when it won't be, then the patient will feel more alone with his problem than before. He is forced to cope, alone, with his fears and anxieties, just when he needs as much help as he can get. Many patients, of course, do not want to know the truth, and this wish should be respected. But for those who do, and most patients do want to know the worst, it is unfair to deceive them. Psychologists and clergymen have said that to mislead elderly people about approaching death is to degrade and ridicule them. "A man who has handled his own affairs with maturity for sixty or seventy years," observed the *United Synagogue Review*, "has the right to face the end without being treated like a stupid child." A Roman Catholic bishop, John J. Wright, once remarked that friends do a great injustice to a dying person by denying him an opportunity to prepare for the transition from this world to eternal life. "In the case of those who see death as the turning of a page," he said, "the opening of a door, or in any sense a commencement rather than a conclusion, strong considerations of morality and a decent regard for their presumed preferences require that doctors or others decently inform them of the nearness of death."

The fear of dying alone is greater than any other fear, it has been said. How the dying person handles the situation he finds himself in depends, in large measure, on the attitude of those around him. Someone must share his pain and fear while he is allowed to cling to some small piece of the world he has known. Dr. Samuel L.

Feder, a psychiatrist at Mount Sinai Hospital in New York, has put it aptly: "While there is little a doctor can do to help a person to die, there is much he can do to help a person to live until the time of death."

Take the case of Tommy, a seventeen-year-old boy suffering from leukemia. His parents were told by the doctor that nothing could be done medically for him, that he would die in a year. Tommy knew, too. At the beginning, it was hard to accept, but Tommy's family, including two brothers and a sister, was always a close one. And so they continued on as usual, as nearly as possible. They held dinner parties, vacationed in Europe, went to ball games and movies together. Tommy's condition worsened, but, with the help of medication to dull some of his pain, they stuck it out. Above all, they never denied Tommy's problem. They discussed it often, shared it, accepted it. And when the end finally came for Tommy, it was difficult, but not as hard as it might have been had the family given in to the natural inclination, "What's the use?" Tommy's mother said later, "It was an experience we'll never forget, one that, under the circumstances, was the most rewarding we'd ever had together. It's drawn us closer, if such a thing is possible, and the opportunity to care for Tommy and to share his suffering was a blessing, for him and for us."

Several programs aimed at exploring what is called the "psychology of death" have been undertaken. One of the most important has been at the University of Chicago. An "instructor" who is actually a patient dying of an illness sits behind a one-way glass partition and talks to doctors, medical students and nurses, many of whom have never before discussed what death means. The patient volunteers to share his personal feelings, hopes and despairs as death nears. Dr. Elizabeth K. Ross, an assistant professor of psychiatry, began the program several years ago when four theology students decided to conduct a study on death as a crisis in human life. They started from scratch. The first patient approached was extremely ill, and so angry that he took it out on everyone. Nurses hated to go near him. Nevertheless, the man wanted to talk, and as he began to express himself, Dr. Ross found out why he was angry. "He had so much to say," she explained, "and no one had been willing to really sit down and listen."

Over the years, Dr. Ross has talked to hundreds of terminal patients, ranging in age from the teens to the nineties. Each of the patients volunteers to "teach" the students, and the seminar often serves also as therapy for the dying person, as well as a learning experience for the professionals. Dr. Ross's work has revealed that almost all dying patients go through a number of common psychological stages. At first, the patient experiences a great emotional shock when he hears the diagnosis that he will die soon. Then he denies the seriousness of the illness. He will say, "No, the doctors have the wrong slide, the wrong X-ray interpretation. It cannot be me." Eventually, the patient accepts his condition. But he becomes angry and tries to punish the staff and his own family for the illness. The more people try to help, the angrier he grows. The patient then enters what Dr. Ross calls the "bargaining stage." During this period, he will often plead, "If only I could be free of this pain for one day more, then I would die in peace." This is followed by deep depression, until finally the patient reaches a period of acceptance just before death. This acceptance, according to Dr. Ross, is the hardest time for the family because relatives usually do not reach this phase simultaneously with the patient. The patient may want to be alone, to die in peace, but the family finds it difficult to accept this. They become frantic, and they ask doctors if they can do another operation, find some cure, anything to reverse the inevitable. "In this way," says Dr. Ross, "they are unwittingly destructive."

It is Dr. Ross's contention that fear of death in America is especially strong because people rarely see death. They can avoid it. It becomes a mechanical operation, something that is nice and clean and sterile, something that takes place in a modern hospital. This fear of death, she believes, extends itself to physicians and nurses with the result that the dying patient often is not seen as an ordinary human being who has great emotional needs as well as physical ones.

Some of Dr. Ross's colleagues have felt her work is sad and depressing, but she does not. Her feelings have been expressed this way: "To me, this is a most gratifying, most rewarding experience. These terminally ill people have been neglected. They have so much to give, and so much to teach the rest of us. If only young doctors learn to impart hope to the dying, and to commit themselves fully to helping these people, then they have learned a great deal from the seminars."

Another expert on the dying patient is Dr. Melvin J. Krant, Director of the Oncology Division (a branch of science dealing with tumors) at the Tufts-affiliated Lemuel Shattuck Hospital in Boston. Dr. Krant is co-founder of the Equinox Institute, an organization created to promote better understanding of death, dying and bereavement. At the Shattuck Hospital, efforts are made to ease the pain of terminally ill patients and treat their disease. But also, the staff pays close attention to the psychological and social status of both patient and his family. Regular family meetings are held in the evening, and family members are invited to meet with the staff on a regular basis in a bereavement clinic. Interviews are held with the patients and families, sometimes separately and sometimes together, and the issue of death and dying is allowed to be raised openly by patient and family. If patients die on the unit, open discussion between patients and staff is encouraged in relationship to such losses.

"To care for an individual with a terminal illness is to become aware of the meaning of disintegration and dying as seen on personal spiritual terms, on psychologic terms and on social terms," says Dr. Krant. "It also requires the recognition that there are many tasks in the care of such an individual which may be better performed by nurses, social workers or other non-physician health care personnel, but working together with the physician as peer-givers rather than as subordinates. It also is to be recognized that terminal care may be better administered outside of institutions, if services can so be arranged to give support to the family. And it must be eminently clear that the impact of terminal illness and of dying is not just on patients and the care-giving staff, but on various family members who may be scarred and mutilated by such an event for an indefinite time into the future."

Dr. Krant takes issue with the view of a "fitting death" as simply the exhaustion of medical efforts to keep a patient alive longer. Such a concept, he suggests, implies that death is never appropriate or fitting and that the health care staff must always look at the dying patient as a failure of their efforts. "An attitude of this nature prevents the creation of those very necessary services which can bring about a fitting and appropriate death," he explains, "and a fitting and appropriate effort to assist families in working through their grief reactions. The concept of a fitting death as brought about through a disease process, rather than a moralistic or heroic process, is the gradual biologic decline of human life in a relatively calm psychologic equilibrium in which personal dignity is maintained and a consensus exists between the doctor, the health care staff, the patient and the relatives that everything possible has been done for the patient, but that death remains inevitable. Such a concept implies that peaceful resignation of impending death by the patient and by his family, and the acceptance of this inevitability by the health care staff."

It is unfortunate, says Dr. Krant, that such circumstances are seldom reached today. The incurable cancer patient often is moved from one therapeutic service to another, is cared for by many physicians, and finds it difficult to view anyone as his own personal doctor. "Much cancer care is administered in institutions which may not be geared to studying the interactions between patient and family, nor to understanding the dependency and patterns of communication which naturally have existed and continue to exist between certain family members," the doctor adds. "In the busy rush to apply technologic medicine to the alleviation of the patient's problems, it is not infrequent that the patient as a psychologic, sociologic and individualistic organism is overlooked. At times, there is an overt necessity for the physician to avoid understanding the patient as a human with behavioral aspects, because the threat of disease is so overwhelming that the physician is either uncomfortable or frightened, and indeed is untrained to deal with that individual as a complex structure over and above his biologic behavior."

In an effort to change the way in which terminal care is now delivered and taught, the Shattuck's oncology unit has been working closely with the psychiatry department at Tufts Medical School. This joint approach is aimed, among other things, at returning the care of the dying individual to his family in his community but with the backup support of medical facilities. It seeks to develop educational patterns for health-care professionals around issues of dying and bereavement. And it hopes to develop interinstitutional and community-based programs to remove the taboo nature of the subject of death in society and to openly arrange for more intimate caretaking by families and other community people for those with serious chronic and terminal diseases.

"As long as the family feels that it can cope with their loved individual and that services in the form of nursing and medicine are available to deal with issues as they arise," says Dr. Krant, "security in giving terminal care at home is frequently observed. This does not mean that all families are capable of providing such care, either due to economic and work needs, psychologic distortions, previous patterns of behavior or other reasons. In such cases, the program does not insist on forcing terminal care at home but allows back-up facilities at the hospital to be used when indicated."

Another study of deathbed attitudes and behavior — focusing on elderly patients — was conducted a few years ago by Dr. Robert Kastenbaum, former director of psychological research at Cushing Hospital in Framingham, Massachusetts, and now director of the Center for Psychological Studies of Dying, Death and Lethal Behavior at Wayne State University in Detroit. Employing a technique called the "psychological autopsy" — in which the preterminal and terminal phases of a recently deceased patient are reconstructed — Dr. Kastenbaum, along with Dr. Avery Weisman of the Massachusetts General Hospital, reported at a meeting of the Gerontological Society that the study failed to support the commonly held assumption that old people generally lose contact with reality when they are dying. In the cases studied, nineteen patients were classified as accepting death. What they said and did during the preterminal period appeared to be strongly influenced by recognition that death was near and by a general attitude of acceptance or readiness for it. One ninety-year-old woman, described as alert and independent, made arrangements for her own funeral when her health began to fail. She said she had lived her life and was ready for its end. She refused medication, and insisted that any attempt to prolong her life would be a crime.

Sixteen patients were classified as having been "interrupted by death." These people recognized that death was nearing, but continued to participate in daily life, planning new projects and experiences. In this group was an eighty-two-year-old woman who, when admitted to the hospital, appeared resigned to death and even expressed a desire for it. Later on, she became involved in the institution's social and recreational life. After three years, said Dr. Kastenbaum, she faced death as though it were a regrettable interruption of her activities and interpersonal relationships. Patients and staff members at the hospital felt the same way. They regarded her impending death as a loss to the hospital community.

A few years back, Dr. Herman Feifel, chief psychologist at the Veterans Administration Hospital Outpatient Clinic in Los Angeles, conducted another survey of attitudes toward death and dying. This one contrasted the feelings of a group of ninety-two seriously or terminally ill patients with those of ninety-five healthy, normal persons. Among the things Dr. Feifel found out was that a belief in divine God and an afterlife was more common among the sick. In contrast, the healthy saw God not so much as divine but as a "greater power." The patients also denied ideas of suicide. When they were asked how they would not want to die, the response was "not violently." The healthy individuals, on the other hand, seemed to be more afraid of a long, lingering death. Some possible explanations of this might be that the patients were disavowing their situation, and that they wished to keep their bodies intact and whole because of a strong belief in an afterlife. Also, according to the psychiatrist, their disapproval of violent death may have hidden above-average feelings of hostility toward themselves and others.

The same study found that although fear of the unknown dominated death attitudes of all the subjects, the fear of being separated from family and loved ones was more prominent in the patients. Younger patients, as expected, were more apt to reject death than the older ones. Subjects who had known about their impending death for six months or more were less afraid than those who had just learned of it. "Even the most dreaded reality," reported Dr. Feifel, "apparently responds to the law of familiarity."

In another study by Dr. Kastenbaum, a number of housewives were interviewed. Some looked at death with calm acceptance, others with a strong faith in immortality. They were asked to visit a group of hospital patients. Some were terminal cases. Despite the women's views on death, Dr. Kastenbaum found that all managed to draw near to and talk openly with those who were simply sick, but moved away from and hardly looked at those they thought were dying.

The great psychoanalyst Sigmund Freud was one who feared death early in his life. He was preoccupied with the idea that he might die at various ages: forty-two, sixty-two and eighty-one, the last being the age at which his father and older brother had died. Later, through his own self-analysis, Freud managed to fight his fear, and although references to death and aging show up in his letters, these have been taken to reveal a contempt of aging which could drain his creative energy, and not a continued fear of death. Freud was eighty-three when he died.

Fear of death, one study has revealed, appears to be more intense in the disturbed of young and middle age. Dr. Karl Achte, of the psychiatric clinic of the University of Helsinki Central Hospital, interviewed 178 persons. A third were emotionally healthy young adults; a third were young and middle-aged disturbed persons; and another third were old people, of whom half were psychically healthy. According to Dr. Achte, a fear of death was shown in 24 per cent of the total. None of the healthy old people, and only 17 per cent of the healthy young, displayed it. He found that 67 per cent of the total preferred sudden death. The proportion, again, was highest (78 per cent) in the group of disturbed young and middle-aged subjects, and lowest in the group of old people. Also, Dr. Achte found, euthanasia, or "mercy killing," was deemed admissible by 48 per cent of the subjects studied. Those most in favor of putting to death a patient suffering from an incurable disease were the healthy young (62 per cent), and those most opposed were the old persons (57 per cent).

A fear of death depends on a number of things. Our cultural and religious beliefs, our attitudes toward life and the living, and our general emotional health all play a role. Physicians, it is said, are more afraid of death than their patients. Why this is supposed to be so is not quite clear. It may be the closeness to death that is so much a part of the doctor's job. Or it may be that they unconsciously brought the fear of death to medicine, choosing such a specialty in the first place as a means of denying that death is a threat. Some medical students are said to be overly concerned about their own health and well-being, and this attitude, according to psychiatrists, goes along with a fear of death. These ideas, of course, are but generalities, and there are numerous other reasons why men and women elect to become doctors.

A strong upbringing in a religious faith that faces death head-on and offers a resurrection of the body and life everlasting can calm fears or make them worse, depending on one's personal makeup. For some, the promise of eternal reward is enough to allay the fear of dying. A world of happiness and rest awaits them, provided they play by rules which not only insure them a place in eternity but which help keep the world on a decent path. There is nothing to lose in "being good," some reason, because if the moral life is followed, both society and the individual benefit. If there is no hereafter, there obviously is nothing to worry about. "There are just two alternatives with regard to death," said Socrates. "Either the dead man has lost all power of perception, and wholly ceased to be; or else, as tradition has it, the soul at death changes its habitation, moving from its home here to its home yonder. And if there is no perception at all, and death is like a sound sleep, unbroken even by a dream, then it is a wonderful gain." For those who do not believe in an afterlife, there is little fear. They can take comfort in leaving a good memory of themselves behind for relatives and friends. Or, they can live for themselves alone, trying to enjoy life to the fullest, with or without regard for anyone else.

There are those whose fear of death is overwhelming, even with a strong religious background. These are the overly scrupulous individuals, laymen and clergymen, who cannot accept the fact that their lives have not been perfect. A layman who thinks this way treads an especially difficult path. On the one hand, he tries to lead a totally spiritual, all-good, church-governed life; on the other, he tries to stay in the mainstream of every-day life, a course full of responsibilities, interests and temptations. Were he a monk in an isolated monastery, a wholly religious existence, although difficult, would be an ordinary one. In his attempt to lead an extraordinary life in a sinful world, conflict arises. He deeply fears eternal damnation, believing strongly that such will be his lot.

Some people, influenced by bizarre literature, ignorant individuals or by some mental deficiency, have fears of being cut loose in an unknown and bleak spirit world in their own or another form, or worse, being buried alive. Carried further, some even dread an after-life of peace. Such an experience is seen as a bore, a drag, by those who live to do, and they shudder at the thought of one day being inactive forever and ever.

Somewhere between those whose faith sustains them and those whose absence of faith serves the same purpose lie most of us. Unsure what is "on the other side," we are apprehensive about dying and we remain so until we teach ourselves to live comfortably with the thought. This does not mean that we should be preoccupied with death. Some people think of little else as they prepare for it, ponder on it, worry over it. This can be worse than total denial of death. A look over our shoulders now and then, however, a casual glance at the future, is a healthy thing, a habit that will help us shape our lives.

Premonitions of death often accompany preoccupation, and there are many classic examples of this. Thrice in her sleep did Calphurnia cry out, "Help, ho! They murder Caesar." Two days before he was assassinated, Abraham Lincoln had a dream about his death. And the composer Mozart, at the age of thirty-five, spoke of his death a few months before it came. Many patients, it was pointed out earlier, know they are dying. Their premonitions of death might come merely from watching the reactions of friends and relatives, looking into the doctor's eyes, listening to what nurses say. But whether or not a forewarning of death can occur in persons who are not ill is debatable. It is known, however, that some older people do show psychological changes before death takes them. According to one researcher, Dr. Morton A. Lieberman of the University of Chicago Medical School, they demonstrate definite intellectual and emotional changes about a year before death occurs. He tested eighty persons between the ages of seventy and ninety-five, and of forty who died thirty-four showed a distinct awareness of signs of death. "There was no evidence in these psychological changes that these people had any increased concern or fear," he said, "only that they were monitoring signs within themselves that became symbolized as death." The "psychology of death," Dr. Lieberman added, may begin in middle age. People start to cope with the problem in their late fifties. By the time they are quite old, the majority have come to terms with the situation.

Up to this point, we have been looking at the attitudes of dying patients, and at some of our own feelings about dying and death. It has been noted that terminal patients go through a period of denial, and that healthy individuals do the same thing when the topic of their inevitable death arises. Attention was called to the idea that people don't talk about death because they see so little of it. Many parents, who want their children to know all about sex, go to great lengths to shield them from death, refusing to take them to funerals or wakes, and generally avoiding the subject. The fact is that more than half the deaths in the United States occur in hospitals, and a good proportion of the rest in nursing homes,

homes for the elderly and state mental institutions. Three-fourths of all deaths, then, probably occur in places other than in the home. In other parts of the world, where many people die at home, the attitude is different. "They remain in a familiar environment, in their own bed, surrounded by family," says Dr. Ross. "Most important, perhaps, the children are not sent away. They are permitted to share in some of the responsibilities, caring for the dying person, and in the preparatory grief. They see animals, and sometimes people, born; they see them die. They learn from early childhood that life has a natural beginning and a natural end."

The denial of our own deaths is the same kind of denial we summon up when a loved one dies. Grieving, we lean on euphemisms, and we say things like "He's passed away" or "She's with the angels" or "She's sleeping." We might comfort ourselves and others with such remarks as "It's all for the best" or "His suffering is over" or "She lived a good life, even though it was short."

Most studies of grief and mourning agree that the mourner goes through several stages, much as does the patient who is told he will die soon. The first of these is extreme shock, disbelief and helplessness. This is followed by a period of violent, heartrending grief, a period in which the mourner is completely disorganized. The final period is one of slow acceptance, in which the mourner begins to pull out of his depression. He reorders his life, begins to take an interest in the world again. Normal acute grief lasts anywhere from four to eight weeks. It may also be delayed, coming on months or years later. Or, it can recur on anniversaries of the death.

Grief manifests itself in many ways. The mourner may become preoccupied with the image of the dead person. He may feel guilty for not doing enough for the deceased during life. He may become angry at the doctor who might have helped, or even at the deceased for "deserting" the family. (The anger of grief is unconscious. The mourner becomes tense when a loved one dies. He sees the tension as anger, but such an idea is repulsive. Because such anger is unacceptable, it is transformed into grief and despair.)

Grief can cause many physical and emotional reactions. "A significant number of individuals develop rather marked alterations in their health consequent to a badly resolved grief reaction," says Dr. Krant. "Physical disorders such as asthma, ulcerative colitis, rheumatoid arthritis, cancer, leukemia and many others have been reported as developing as a late consequence of a grief reaction. Certainly, there is little doubt that many psychiatric diseases, especially in the affective disorders, as manic depressive psychosis and psychoneuroses, have been reported as being more frequent in patients undergoing early maternal or paternal losses than in control populations. The field of suicide constantly warns us to be aware of somebody who has suffered loss that has not been resolved, for such individuals are highly at risk for committing suicide. Juvenile delinquency, school dropouts, drug abuse, are all seen as having a high order of frequency resulting from loss and abandonment reactions."

In general, however, grief must be recognized as normally self-limiting, a universal human experience. Freud said normal grief is resolved by reality, and that any interference with it is useless. Reaction to bereavement is rarely seen by the psychiatrist, and the chances are that those who seek psychiatric help to help them adjust to the death of a loved one were suffering from some emotional disorder to begin with.

Whether grief can kill has not been satisfactorily established. Down through the ages, poets, lovers and balladeers have repeated the plaintive refrain — that a broken heart can put an end to one's life. A few years ago, after the death of former Congo Premier Moise Tshombe, a diplomat who knew him well surmised he died of loneliness and a broken heart. In an effort to find out whether such an occurrence is romantic fallacy or fact, a British study which stretched over nine years revealed that during the first six months of bereavement, the death rate among widowers was 40 per cent higher than expected. The study also determined that nearly half the deaths were due to heart disease. Writing in the *British Medical Journal*, Dr. C. Murray Parkes noted that it was possible that emotional stress acted by altering the consumption of fats, sugars, coffee or tobacco. All of these have been shown to be statistically related to mortality from heart disease. Dr. Parkes said also that in a few cases, emotional stress alone might be enough to cause death. This is so since it causes changes in pulse rate, blood pressure and cardiac output. The investigators added that should the patient have a preexisting hypertension (high blood pressure) or heart disease, such changes could have a disastrous effect. In another study in Great Britain, it was found that the mortality rate of survivors who participated in the terminal care of family members at home was less than half the rate of survivors who lost a family member in a hospital or other institution. "The resolution of the meaning of death and participation in family structure during the dying process," says Dr. Krant, "may well be a potent force in determining health patterns of those who continue living." So, in one sense, it is possible that a "broken heart" can cause death.

Most physicians agree that the key to handling a grief crisis is, first, to assure the mourner that his situation is not unique. Second, he must be encouraged to talk about his grief because it is better to free one's pent-up emotions. At a conference on religion and medicine held in conjunction with the 1970 annual meeting of the American Medical Association, the Reverend Granger E. Westberg of Wittenberg University noted: "One of the tasks of the minister and the doctor is to teach people in advance of their 'earthshaking' loss that they must work through their grief, that grief is normal, it is healthy, it has healing qualities, it can actually be 'good grief.'" When a person is in a state of grief, he explained, he must be made to see that an adjustment to a new way of life is necessary. "We affirm reality. We can say that in some ways our grief experiences have been good."

Dr. Paul S. Rhoads of Chicago, who also spoke at the conference, summed up the role of the family physician in times of grief by saying, "Patients with grievous and often terminal illness, as well as their families who are suffering with them, are entitled to all the sympathy and understanding and support we can give them. . . . Those we serve do not expect miracles from us, much as they hope for them. But they do expect understanding and sympathy bestowed with the dignity that all human relationships should have."

Funeral rites, wakes and periods of mourning help us face death in a direct way. They let us release tensions and readjust. They are as much for us, the living, as for the dead.

Various ceremonies and practices have come down to us from ancient days. They probably sprang out of man's fear of the ghosts of the dead and a determination to appease them by helping them, as much as possible, on their journey through the afterlife. The Greeks, for instance, placed coins in the mouths of the dead so that Charon, the ferryman who carried souls across the river Styx, could be paid. Egyptians mummified their dead kings out of a belief that preservation of the body kept the soul alive. In Africa, various tribes killed wives and slaves after the death of a king so that their souls could minister to his spirit. Cannibalism, practiced in several parts of the world, was a way of keeping in the closest possible touch with the deceased. For this same reason, some American Indians consumed the ashes of their cremated brothers. In India, the Hindu practice of suttee, in which a widow threw herself on her husband's funeral pyre, was common until the British abolished it in 1829.

Mourning customs vary as widely as funeral rites. Wearing black, symbolic of the mysterious night and, therefore, the more fearsome side of death, dates back to the early Romans who also gave us the custom of walking in funeral processions. Roman mourners carried on for nine days, during which time they made offerings at the deceased person's tomb and banqueted royally. At the dying man's last breath, it was customary to call out his name, a practice carried on to this day when a pope dies. Some Australian tribes cut their bodies with stone knives, others paraded backward with their clothing turned inside out because it was believed the hereafter was a world of opposites. In China, where mourners often wear white, there can be much gaiety. In some parts of Europe, on the other hand, clocks are stopped at the hour of death, windows are covered, and the hearth fire is extinguished. In Japan, the family altar with its photograph of the deceased enables the family to adapt to the loss. The dead, according to one report, become ancestors who are fed, given gifts and talked to. In some Latin American countries, family members gather together from great distances to join in mourning with a mother who has lost a newborn infant.

Some people believe that death customs and rituals build up more tensions than they release. Doctors among them might prescribe medicine to relieve the mourner, or might forbid him to attend a wake or funeral. Well-meaning friends might advise, "Don't cry, it'll be all right" or "There, there, it won't do any good to carry on that way." Aside from the fact that the general health of some mourners might require such a cautious approach, it is clear that this attitude denies death — and that is unhealthy. Denial prevents us from adjusting to death when it strikes someone near and dear, and, more important, it fills us with dread when the thought of our own future end crosses our minds. One form of denial shows up in the practice of holding a wake, in which a watch is kept over the body of a dead person before burial. Mourning and facing death are, as has been emphasized, good things. But at the usual American wake the mourner is not allowed to see death as it really is. The body is embalmed to last for years. The face is painted and covered with cosmetics, and a waxen smile is fixed in place. The coffin is ornate and expensive, and, seemingly, comfortable. An important and natural event, the death of a human being, is masked. Death is not like this. It is not always a pleasant sight, but yet it is not something to be hidden under a lifelike disguise. To look at it that way is to neglect it and, therefore, to fear it.

We still have a good deal to learn about facing death. We must see it as a natural occurrence rather than as a violent accident. We must learn to treasure each minute, each day, each year. "Dying is not so terrible," Dr. Ross has said, "if you have learned through experience that it is part of life." A number of colleges and medical centers have adopted an offbeat approach to help young people come to just that realization. Some make use of a technique known as psychodrama to get students to talk about death and dying. Psychodrama is not acting in the usual sense of the word. The participants act out their problems, and by doing so learn to develop keener insights into their emotional difficulties. By playing roles in dramas involving death, by experiencing it, so to speak, they take a closer look at it, even though it is not real, and hangups about the usually unmentionable subject may be softened. Another way is to expose students to music, poetry and films about death — instead of the standard classroom pattern of dry lectures full of statistics and detached facts followed by an exam — and then allow them to get together in groups either to act out what they have learned, or to discuss their impressions.

We must learn that since life is relatively short, it is better to live it in a springtime way, appreciating each new bud, each newborn babe, each new experience. For when the end comes, as it must for all of us, what will matter is the quality of the life we have lived. The poet Dylan Thomas advised:

> *Do not go gentle into that good night,*
> *Old age should burn and rave at close of day;*
> *Rage, rage against the dying of the light.*

Our life shapes the kind of death we all are destined

to experience. It is our life that will determine whether we will "rage, rage," or whether we will "go gentle into that good night." The great comedian W. C. Fields was one who did not rage out of this world when his time came. He is reported to have quipped on his deathbed, "Well, it's better than being in Philadelphia." Confederate General Robert E. Lee's last words were a military command to break camp: "Strike the tent." And Sam Rayburn the speaker of the U.S. House of Representatives, is said to have told a relative as he lay dying in a hospital room, "This is the damnedest thing that's ever happened to me."

An empty, unfulfilled life will end, almost inevitably, in a meaningless, despairing death. Such a death can be an unbearable, fearful event, a tragedy which the dying person refuses to accept. He feels cheated and angry. Death is a rude interruption, a bad scene, a bummer. But a life that has been full, rewarding and satisfying prepares one for the finale in the best way. For those who can look back on such a life and who have found meaning either in a faith in God or in their fellow man, death itself becomes a sort of fulfillment, a completion, a period that is placed, without regrets, at the end of the story. Some might take comfort in the words of Jesus, who said, "Let not your heart be troubled, for in my Father's house are many mansions." For others, the source of solace might be Marcus Aurelius: "It is not death that man should fear, but he should fear never beginning to live."

To a young person, it might sound strange that an

individual who has led a full and good life could leave it without gnashing his teeth and without feeling he wants to keep it forever. It is true, of course, that the majority of us do not want to die — those of us who have had a life of gratification as well as those who have not. And the untimely death of a young person — in an accident, in war or by suicide — is not easily accepted. This kind of death that cuts off a life before it has had a chance to prosper and know fulfillment might well be considered a bad death. It would seem that only a deep religious faith and a belief in a God-ordained plan can ease its sting. What is at issue is not whether we do or do not want to die. "All men," said Victor Hugo, "are condemned to death. It is only the date of execution that is uncertain." Since we have nothing to say about the matter, it is the way we look at death that is important. And what seems certain is that how we go out of the world depends heavily on how we've lived in it.

"As a well-spent day brings happy sleep," remarked Leonardo da Vinci, "so a well-spent life brings happy death."

Four

Euthanasia

Few people can appreciate fully how deeply the human heart can be touched at the agony a suffering and incurable individual experiences: a son distressed over his bedridden father whose body is full of tubes to keep him alive, a mother in a deep depression over her retarded child, a doctor asking himself again and again whether it is right for him to take unusual measures to maintain the life of a very old patient afflicted with a painful and incurable cancer, a patient with no home, no family, no friends.

Often, individuals take it upon themselves to put sufferers — pain-wracked incurables, the hopelessly insane, those living out an artificial "vegetable" existence with the aid of machines and medications, or the aged — out of their misery. Such an act, popularly known as "mercy killing," is euthanasia (from the Greek words *eu*, meaning good or well, and *thanatos*, death). A physician might perform one kind of euthanasia by administering a heavy dose of a potent drug, either on his own best judgment without the patient's consent, at the pleading of the patient himself, or on request of a relative. Or he may perform another kind of euthanasia by omitting acts that would prolong the life of the sufferer: he could, for instance, withhold oxygen, drugs or emergency treatment, reasoning that he has no moral obligation to take extraordinary means to save an incurable patient who is in excruciating pain. The young mother might murder her defective child, convinced in her despair that she was performing a true act of mercy. Or, as in the concluding scene of the film *They Shoot Horses, Don't They?* a young man fires a fatal shot into the head of his disillusioned dance partner and, in the only explanation he can offer for the deed, utters the movie's title words.

Direct euthanasia, the deliberate act of ending a suffering person's life, is not legally sanctioned in any civilized country. The law, grounded as it is on life's sanctity, holds that no human being has the right to take another's life — unless he acts in self-defense, as an instrument of the state in the execution of a condemned criminal, or in a just war. If you take your own life, you are guilty of suicide; if someone does it for you, be he friend or physician, relative or stranger, he is guilty of murder. Acts of passive euthanasia, in which a doctor elects *not* to do something that might prolong life or a suffering patient refuses to take the medicine that will maintain him, probably are more common and undoubtedly go on behind the scenes more often than realized. (We will examine this form in depth later on since it is a more relevant issue in modern-day discussions of death and dying.)

The "mercy killings" which have caught the public eye have almost always been of a violent or dramatic nature. And there have been many of them. In Michigan in the 1920's, a man on trial for the murder of his wife told the court that the woman, suffering from an incurable disease, asked him to leave a cup of an arsenic mixture near her bed. He did so. She drank the poison and died. His conviction of first degree murder was upheld by the state's supreme court. In 1938, a woman osteopath from Miami poisoned her incurably ill daughter, then tried to kill herself. In a suicide note she explained: "Barbara is sick. I don't want her to stay behind and suffer. I am too tired and sick to hold on." In 1939, a prosperous, middle-aged man, after months of soul-searching indecision, killed his seventeen-year-old son because he was an incurable imbecile. While police of the emergency squad tried vainly to revive the boy, the father remarked, "I hope you don't bring him back. He's better off." In Versailles, France, there was the strange trial of four nurses charged with the mercy killing of seven incurables; the hospital had been ordered evacuated because German forces were advancing and the patients could not be transported. In 1945, a thirty-one-year-old American lieutenant colonel in the Air Force was charged with voluntary manslaughter when he allegedly fired two pistol shots to end the agony of a sergeant gunner pinned in the burning wreckage of a B–25 bomber. He was acquitted.

To the proponents of euthanasia, these acts are reasonable ones, justified on the ground that concern for the sufferer is of the utmost importance; to opponents, they are crimes against man and God.

Generally speaking, euthanasia advocates believe strongly in the right of an incurably diseased person to have his life ended gently. While few today favor it on a compulsory basis, proponents feel it is inhuman to refuse the request of a sufferer that he be eased into death or allowed to die by withholding treatment. Extreme suffering, they reason, degrades and demoralizes, thereby forcing life to lose its meaning. To them, the value of life is qualitative, and not a quantitative thing — that is, it is better to live a meaningful existence, to self and community, than merely to live it. They point out that physicians who refuse a mercy death to a pleading, hopeless individual are placing a tremendous emotional and financial burden on the family of the sufferer as well as on society. They argue that when a man has become a "vegetable," with hope of recovery gone, it is as immoral to maintain him at a cost of, say, thirty thousand dollars a year in a hospital bed that could be used by other sick people as it is to allow him to die, or to induce his death. Physicians, the advocates believe, are bound to heal, but they also are bound to relieve pain, particularly pain that is tied to an incurable disease that drags a sufferer down a one-way street, tearing apart his personality and destroying life's essence. Euthanasia is a more urgent issue now that life may be extended by medical science, simply because man is more subject to the prolongation of his pain. Voluntary euthanasia for incurables, they sum up, is compatible with moral and religious principles, and should be established as an additional human value; pain, when the sufferer is on a last mile, has no soul-saving nor character-building value.

Opponents of euthanasia cite the commandment

"Thou shalt not kill," maintaining that mercy killing is only a euphemism for murder and only God, not man, has absolute control over life. God, in effect, is the property-owner, man only the housekeeper. (Euthanasia advocates will argue that if this is true, then it is equally wrong to lengthen life by medical means since this, too, is tampering.) For some Christians, suffering is not an absolute evil and may have its redeeming side. This argument likens the torment of the sufferer to the white heat of a forge, and the elevation of spirit and closeness to God it can bring to the fine steel that emerges. Pope Pius XII, while pointing out that the sick and dying are not obliged to suffer, noted, "If some dying persons accept suffering as a means of expiation and a source of merits in order to go forward in the love of God and in abandonment to His will, do not force anesthetics upon them. They should rather be aided to follow their own way." (Suffering, the Pope admitted, may also furnish occasion for new faults, and in some cases it would be inadvisable to suggest that a dying person follow that route toward salvation.) In place of the argument that pain is an absolute evil, euthanasia opponents offer the conclusion that the whole concept of suffering has been blown out of proportion, that often it is the relative of the sufferer who is suffering and that it really is he who wishes to be relieved; his motive may be stated as humanitarian, but actually is selfish since he wishes to relieve himself of the burden. Also, new drugs and techniques for the relief of pain are continually coming into daily use, and there are few cases where pain cannot be alleviated.

Opponents raise a number of other strong objections. Extending to man the argument that we put an animal out of its misery, they say, implies that there is no essential difference between animal and man. The physician who performs euthanasia, with or without the patient's consent, may have erred in his diagnosis, and the patient might not have been as hopelessly ill as assumed. The possibility of science's discovering new cures for the incurable is another point. There also is the argument that to discuss disease in such terms as incurable is to admit defeat, and that to employ euthanasia is surrender. And what of the sufferer who begs for death today and changes his mind tomorrow or a week later? What of the conniving relative who might inherit the wealth of the dying patient? To whom would the euthanasia advocates give the right to kill whom? What protection would there be against crimes committed under the name of mercy? And lastly, would a society with a euthanasia law on its books — ostensibly for humanitarian reasons — be able to resist the temptation to do away with the aged, the inefficient or those whose ideas represent a threat to the ruling class?

Those ranged on both sides of the matter can point to a number of cases which lend support to their views. The following, while it might be used to buttress the anti-euthanasia position, also serves to focus attention on the frame of mind of a sufferer who has lost hope. Consider the case of Mrs. Sarah Harris, a thirty-three-year-old paralytic, who, in 1912, begged the state of New York to put an end to her life. From her bed in a sanitarium, the woman, mother of two small children whom she refused to see again because she did not wish them to be aware of her suffering, dictated a letter, with the request that it be sent to the newspapers:

"Can the busy throng stop long enough from their various avocations in life to consider a most vital question from one of the greatest sufferers who inhabits this beautiful world?" Mrs. Harris asked. "One question, the greatest of all, how to end the suffering of hopeless, helpless sufferers, has never been delved into. Masterminds of medical science, skilled diagnosticians, have exhausted their efforts in bringing about some relief or cure for me. Now why should not the state take the matter in its hands and end the wretchedness of such poor sufferers? Let us just stop long enough to think that when a brute, the lowliest of the animal kingdom, becomes inactive and doomed to suffer, its suffering is put to an end. And here, a human being, the highest and noblest of created things, must linger and suffer on until the vital organs give way, which may be an indefinite number of years. What a cruel order of the universe."

Later, Mrs. Harris told a reporter: "There is not one thing on earth which could give me the faintest sensation of pleasure. Before I was ill, one of my greatest enjoyments was reading. Now I could not turn the page of a book. My suffering is too intense to let me listen while another reads aloud. No power can make life

63

easier for me. The one thing I can look forward to is death."

The heart-wringing appeal was widely discussed, and opinions were mixed over whether she should be granted her request. Those closest to her continued to hold out hope that, with some advance of medicine, her health might be restored or her suffering lessened.

During the public outcry that arose, euthanasia advocates called opponents hypocrites for condoning killing in war but not for the suffering and dying. And when Dr. Henry Lloyd, superintendent of the hospital in which the woman was bedridden, declared that she might live for ten or twenty years, a great many people expressed the opinion that it was actually unmerciful for the law to forbid ending her life.

A strong argument against euthanasia was offered at the time by Dr. Britton Evans, medical director of the New Jersey State Hospital and an expert on mental diseases. In a statement that is embraced by opponents to this day, Dr. Britton said that euthanasia was not justifiable under any circumstances, and that while it might be considered humane by some, the precedent would be extremely harmful. "The dark stain on the life of Napoleon," he said, "and the one that lost him many potential admirers, was the accusation that he was in the habit of putting suffering soldiers out of the way. The function of a physician is to restore and prolong life. To take it away would be turning from his duty toward society. The effect of such a practice on the body politic would be such as the medical profession could not well risk, nor could any governing body undertake the responsibility of saying who would be chloroformed and who not. It is too much power to bestow upon any man or group of men."

His views were echoed by Dr. Elwood Kirby, an authority on cancer, who said: "Such cases are very pathetic. But to put into the hands of one doctor or a board of doctors the legal right to determine when a human life should be taken would be conferring too great an authority. There would be too many opportunities to take advantage of what might be considered a good and humane law. Of course, there are many cases where several doctors could agree that the disease was incurable, but to arrive at an opinion as to the time when life should be taken would be difficult."

Mrs. Harris's case had a relatively happy ending. A year later, a physician who was visiting the sanitarium dropped in to talk with her. He asked her the history of her case, and when she told him about it replied, "As sure as I'm a walking man, you'll be a walking woman." An operation was performed which relieved her of the intense pain, and later she was able to move a bit and sit in a wheelchair. The encouraging words and the easing of her pain brought about a change in Mrs. Harris's attitude. She admitted that it had been the calmly rendered verdict of her doctors that she had no chance that caused her to cry for euthanasia. Though she did not have complete control of her body, she said, her mind was free and she would write short stories. She summed up her new outlook with these words: "When I asked for euthanasia I would have hailed it as a welcome deliverance. Now I shudder to think what might have happened had such a law been enacted."

The controversy over euthanasia is one that has raged for centuries, and it probably will continue to be hotly debated for many years to come. Apart from those who would deal with it in a passive way, proponents vary in how strongly they feel about it. One group favors euthanasia on a *voluntary* basis for the dying and the incurable. A dying patient, they feel, should have the option of requesting, and a physician should be allowed to administer, say, a fatal overdose of a drug. Another group is for *compulsory* euthanasia, but would limit it to the physically deformed or mentally defective in the early stages of life. Others would add the insane, all incurables and the aged. Extremists would do away with all they consider to be useless and who do not fit their own standards of perfection.

Compulsory euthanasia aimed at ridding a society of the useless, the aged and the infirm, or at bringing about improvement in the type of offspring produced (a concept known as eugenics), was not unknown in the ancient world. In Sparta, defective children were hurled to their deaths from Mount Taygetus. Plato counseled that the offspring of unlicensed matings or the deformed should be left to die. "Let there be a law," wrote Aristotle, "that no deformed child shall be reared." In A.D. 50, Pliny the Elder, a Roman historian and philosopher, noted: "The bounty of Providence has filled the world with herbs for painless death."

In various primitive societies, the aged were considered worthless and, in some cases, were done away with when they lost their capacity to do heavy work. Among the Comanche Indians, warriors did not prepare for old age, reasoning that it was better to be killed in battle. In ancient Fiji, it was supposedly the duty of a devoted son to watch his father carefully, and to kill him when he showed signs of growing senile or decrepit. In the wilds of Labrador, a wandering tribe known as the Montagnais was reported to dispose of their aged and insane by shooting them with bullets cast from melted-down lead crucifixes given them by missionaries, a practice carried on until the 1920's. One newspaper account quoted a young Indian who had just dispatched an elderly member of the tribe: "He no good. He eat all food. Shoot him, and all right now." And in what was the Anglo-Egyptian Sudan, the Nuba tribesmen, convinced that an evil spirit dwelt in the bodies of the lame, the deaf and the dumb, marched their victims out of the village in a procession headed by a goat wearing a brass bell. Both victim and goat were buried alive. (In 1946, police arrested twenty-two tribesmen for murder.)

The idea of relieving society of the burden of elderly people cropped up in this country in 1939. A retired Army officer proposed that persons over 70 who had no means of support should be humanely killed, along with the hopelessly insane, the diseased, defective children and first-degree murderers. "I don't advocate taking everyone on relief rolls and giving them a shot," Major Edward L. Dyer told the Washington Society for Philosophical Research, "but euthanasia should be considered in cases of old age where the persons are of no use to themselves or anyone else. As for the criminally insane, I see no reason why they should not be put out of the way and save the expense of keeping them. Society is finding out so many ways to spend money; this might be a way of saving it."

Compulsory death for the unwanted and unproductive, or to better the species, hardly is advocated publicly nowadays, mostly because of the discredited experience of Nazi Germany. In the fall of 1939, Adolf Hitler signed an order calling for the extermination of all persons who were mentally defective or were suffering from an incurable disease. Superintendents of mental institutions were queried about "eligible" patients. By December, several thousand had been led off to euthanasia camps and shot. Later, the gas chamber — which was to be used to murder millions of Jews in Hitler's "final solution to the Jewish question" — replaced the firing squad as a more efficient method of "therapy" for the ailing unfortunates caught up in the dictator's plan for compulsory death for the useless and undesirable. The drastic scheme, Hitler reasoned, would also conserve food and free necessary hospital beds. The program was classified top secret, and friends and relatives of the doomed patients were told only that they had died of some malady. Eventually, word sifted out of the death centers and a public outcry arose when a rumor started that wounded German soldiers and unproductive workers might be done away with. Though it was halted in 1941, some 275,000 persons, many of them Germans, perished.

Some trace the modern euthanasia movement back to 1516, with Thomas More's *Utopia*, a description of an imaginary kingdom where poverty, crime, injustice and other ills did not exist. "If the disease be not only incurable but also full of continual pain and anguish," More wrote, "then the priests and magistrates exhort the man, seeing he is not able to do any duty of life, and by over-living his own life is noisome and irksome to others and grievous to himself: that he will determine with himself no longer to cherish that pestilent and painful disease. And seeing that life is to him but a torment, that he will not be unwilling to die . . . but either despatch himself out of that painful life as out of a prison, or rack of torment, or else suffer himself to be rid of by other. And in so doing they tell him that he shall do wisely, seeing by his death . . . he shall end his pain. And because in that act he shall follow the counsel of priests, that is to say of the interpreters of God's will and pleasure, they show him that he shall do like a Godly and virtuous man. . . . But they cause none such to die against his will, believing this to be an honorable death."

Efforts to gain acceptance of legalized euthanasia in the United States and Great Britain did not begin until the early twentieth century. One of the first attempts was made in Iowa when proponents tried unsuccessfully to bring about a law authorizing the state to put incurables to death. A bill was introduced in England's House of Lords in 1936, the year the British Voluntary Euthanasia Legalization Society was formed; this was promptly denounced in the press as "a measure to legalize murder" and defeated. Two years later, the Reverend Charles Francis Potter, a New York minister, distressed over seeing incurable cancer patients suffer through their last months, organized the Euthanasia Society of America. Dr. Potter issued appeal after appeal for the legalization of euthanasia, charging, in one passionate speech, that religion was responsible for holding back such legislation. "Neither mercy killing nor suicide is expressly forbidden in the Bible," he said. "There is no commandment, 'Thou shalt not kill.' What the Hebrew of that passage says is 'Thou shalt not commit murder,' as every Hebrew scholar knows." He characterized incurables as a worry to relatives and an expense to the state, adding this stern bit of advice: "We ought to have the moral courage to put them out of the way. A little chloroform and it would be all over."

Euthanasia legislation, which would have allowed sufferers to apply for permission for a "merciful death," was defeated in the Nebraska Legislature. In the ensuing years, three petitions aimed at legalizing "merciful release" were presented to the New York State Legislature by committees of physicians, clergymen and voters. Clergymen who supported the measures were roundly criticized by their more conservative colleagues for departing from "the eternal moral law."

In 1952, another petition went to the United Nations, emphasizing the right of incurable sufferers to voluntary euthanasia. (Today, the Euthanasia Society of America and the Euthanasia Educational Fund do not press for legislation legalizing euthanasia, but rather are dedicated to the concept that all men and women have the right to die with dignity. The organizations also insist that the definition of death must be clarified, and that enlightened education of the public will change the implication that euthanasia is morally reprehensible.)

Attitudes toward euthanasia vary from country to country. In Italy, it is considered a crime if the victim is under eighteen or is mentally retarded. Denmark and Holland have a tolerant attitude, and the Swiss draw a line between killing with evil intentions and killing with good intentions. Sweden passed a law in 1964 legalizing passive euthanasia. And in the Soviet Union, euthanasia may be punished by a prison term of up to eight years.

Euthanasia poses a particularly difficult problem for the physician who has been trained to heed the Hippocratic Oath, an ancient set of guidelines often attributed to the Greek physician Hippocrates (460–377 B.C.) which states unequivocally: "To please no one will I prescribe a deadly drug nor give advice which may cause his death."

The International Code of Medical Ethics also cautions that a doctor must always remember he is charged with the preservation of human life "until death." Physicians have been assigned special responsibility for lengthening the number of man's days on earth, and even in wartime continue to heal; the doctor is exempt from killing under the Geneva Convention. In the sick-room, he is the trusted servant of the suffering, the aged, the diseased; he realizes that if he does not do all he can to bolster an ill patient's confidence, he might wipe out the will to get well.

Nevertheless, some doctors reason that if they can accept that it may be moral to end a life in its early stages — as in an abortion — then it is also right to do so when life is entering the final stage, as when a patient is dying of an incurable disease. Some physicians have admittedly given doses of drugs to bring lives of pain to an end. Others, unwilling to take such a drastic step themselves, have left drugs with a patient or his relatives, knowing full well that a fatal dose will be taken by the patient, or administered by the family at its own discretion. Some years ago, a noted Boston doctor asked a meeting of five hundred physicians to raise their hands if they had never practiced euthanasia. Not a hand went up. Addressing another meeting, a practitioner offered this prescription for incurable cancer: "I leave the patients a week's supply of morphine tablets. I tell them, 'One tablet may ease your pain. Two will ease it. But be careful — if you take them all, you won't wake up in the morning.'" Asked later if any of his patients had ever taken a full bottle of tablets, the doctor replied, "I don't know and I cannot say, but some of them were out of their pain the next day. And if that be murder, let the authorities make the most of it."

In 1935, an English doctor admitted taking the lives of five private patients whom he could not cure. "My conscience never pricked me," he said, "and I still carry with me memories of those cases and the happy faces before they died." More recently, another English doctor told a television audience that he had committed two mercy killings. One involved a defective child, which, the physician said, he merely "put aside and left unattended with the inevitable result." The other was a young man whose internal organs were torn away in a wartime air raid. "Without the slightest hesitation," the doctor said, "I gave him a heavy dose of morphine." An Anglican bishop who appeared on the program with the physician noted that mercy killing was wrong but that there was a difference between deliberate killing and death from an overdose of pain-relieving drugs. He said that if a doctor had to give an extra-large dose of such medication to relieve a person of intolerable agony, then he should do so, even though death would follow immediately.

In 1950, the celebrated case of Dr. Hermann N. Sander of Manchester, New Hampshire, created an international stir. Dr. Sander was indicted for killing a fifty-nine-year-old woman hopelessly ill with cancer. She had had hours to live, and had begged for death. The doctor, it was revealed in his records, had injected air into her bloodstream. The state prosecuted him on the charge of killing the woman, and did not go into the presumptive motive for the alleged act. All evidence the state presented was aimed at establishing that the doctor killed the woman, and mercy killing, as the case was labeled in the press, did not enter into the prosecution's arguments. The defense contended that the patient was dead when the air was injected, and that not enough air to cause death was used. In effect, this meant that the defense was based not on the argument that a mercy killing is not murder, but rather that no mercy killing ever took place. The jury accepted this, and Dr. Sander was acquitted. The verdict was approved by the woman's husband and daughter.

The legal history of euthanasia is a hodgepodge of no-indictments, acquittals, convictions with varying sentences, convictions for lesser offenses or verdicts of temporary insanity. The courts hold generally that, although the motive of the slayer is unselfish — or, according to certain ethical standards, "good" — this is not ordinarily recognized as a defense, and the consent or request of the victim does not affect the fact that a homicide has been committed. But, though the law says killing of a person for humanitarian reasons is not excused, punishment, in mercy killing cases usually is dispensed with a light hand. In 1939, Harry C. Johnson, sixty-five years old, of Long Island, was charged with killing his wife after sitting up for five successive nights listening to her pleas that her suffering from stomach cancer be ended. A grand jury refused to indict him. In 1940, Louis Greenfield went on trial in New York, charged with fatally chloroforming his sixteen-year-old imbecile son. He was acquitted. Similar was the case of Louis Repouille, also of New York, charged with using chloroform to put to death his blind, mentally defective son, age thirteen. He was indicted for manslaughter in the first degree, was convicted of a second-degree manslaughter charge with a jury recommendation of clemency. He drew a five- to ten-year suspended sentence, and was placed on probation. There was the case of a Pittsfield, Massachusetts, man who was sentenced to death for killing his defective son. The sentence was commuted to life in prison, and he eventually was freed on parole. In 1950, a jury at Stamford, Connecticut, released twenty-one-year-old Carol Ann Paight, charged with shooting her father, an incurable cancer patient. The jurors found her "temporarily insane."

Other such cases, in which someone does something to end a life of pain, continue to be decided more or less in the defendant's favor, but his act still cannot be justified legally. The law is clear on that point; deliberate acts to take life, regardless of who does the taking and no matter if the reasons involve charity and compassion, are outlawed. What is less clear, however, is the legal and moral standing of an indirect, passive act of euthanasia. Most of the discussion today does not revolve so much around the legalization of active mercy killing, but on whether one may *withhold* some procedure that would artificially prolong life, so that death will come.

The question is a new one in an age when, as we have seen, it now is possible to keep dying patients alive beyond what would have, in the past, been natural death, with the use of highly sophisticated medical equipment, medication and organ transplants. As we have seen, even after clinical death has occurred, a patient can be revived with special methods, and what a doctor does or doesn't do in this crucial period of a patient's existence raises a host of other questions. Whom does he revive? How does he arrive at that conclusion? If it is his intent to allow a patient to die, is not turning off a respirator the same as giving an overdose of a drug to hasten death? How far must the doctor go to prolong life? Must the measures he takes be ordinary or extraordinary ones? Who gets the heart or kidney transplant or machine? In short, may the doctor play God?

As far back as the early years of the twentieth century, medical men were considering the idea of "letting the patient go" as an alternative, when possible, to the more active form of euthanasia, despite the fact that resuscitative techniques were not as effective as those of today. Permitting a person to die is called orthothanasia (a medical term referring to the art and science of normal or natural death and dying) by some. One noted moral theologian, Professor Joseph Fletcher of the Episcopal Theological School in Cambridge, Massachusetts, calls it antidysthanasia, the avoidance of death that comes in a difficult way.

Dr. Fletcher speaks of two forms of passive euthanasia: indirect voluntary, and indirect involuntary. In the first, a patient, while still conscious and mentally competent, might request his physician to use discretion about letting death come. In the second, the patient's wishes might not be known, but the doctors and/or the family decide for him, choosing to stop fighting death. This form, Dr. Fletcher feels, is the most typical and frequent situation.

Where does one draw the line between attempting to

save life and allowing it to die away? The question involves deep medical, moral, legal and social issues. It crops up again and again, and will continue to do so as medical science continues to be successful in warding off death. Organs for transplant are in short supply, and a surgeon must decide who is to get a heart or kidney. It costs twenty-five thousand to fifty thousand dollars to care for a patient on an artificial kidney machine in a hospital center. Between thirty thousand and fifty thousand people die each year in the United States of kidney disease because they cannot get treatment, or because they are not able to handle complex equipment at home. Who gets the machine?

The decision when to quit prolonging life is a difficult one to make. Each case is different, and the physician, who often must assume the burden alone, must carefully consider a number of factors. The age of the patient, the seriousness of his condition, the cost in terms of professional time and effort, the emotional and financial drain on patient and relatives — all of these must be taken into account. The physician must ask — it is unfortunate, but he must ask it — whether the patient is worth trying to save. Will he contribute anything to society if his life is lengthened? Will he be of any use to family or friends? If he is a young alcoholic derelict, close to no one in the world, does he deserve the only available kidney for transplant — or does it go to the elder statesman? The questions are the same, whether the patient is a candidate for a transplant or whether he is being kept alive by a machine and a doctor who must decide when and whether to shut it off.

In the final analysis, the physician who stops his efforts to keep a hopelessly ill patient alive relies heavily on common sense, hoping that he is right. In the majority of the cases, he shuts down the machine because he is not prolonging life so much as he is prolonging the dying period. He rationalizes that he is not shortening life, that he is not killing anyone, that he is not practicing euthanasia. The patient dies naturally, as he would if the extra measures were not taken, and he has a right to die peacefully and with dignity. And there is no dignity in being dependent on a machine that, at best, is only prolonging the agony.

Many physicians, along with Catholic, Protestant and Jewish moralists, agree that it is advisable to let certain patients die. While they do not support direct methods of euthanasia, they go along with both the indirect voluntary and indirect involuntary methods of ending a sufferer's life. In 1957, Pope Pius XII, in proclaiming his church's official position, added one qualification. *Ordinary* means, the Pope declared, must always be used to preserve life; but there is no obligation to employ extraordinary means. Ordinary means have been taken to include treatment that is not excessively expensive, is conveniently obtained and holds reasonable hope for some benefit. Extraordinary generally refers to treatment which does not fit those requirements. Following this guide, physicians who purposely allow hopelessly ill patients to die are not playing God, but are only exercising a wise administrator's judgment.

Some point out the difficulty in distinguishing between ordinary and extraordinary treatment, simply because what is extraordinary now may not be so in the future. Penicillin often is cited as a medication which once was considered extraordinary treatment, and today is used routinely. If the extraordinary can become the ordinary, does the physician have any right to base his decision on such a principle?

Others also argue that there is little difference between direct and indirect acts of euthanasia, that the intention — bringing about the death of a sick person — is the same in both cases. Is the doctor who leaves the medication by the dying patient's bedside, knowing he will take an overdose, as guilty as the physician who administers a poison? Whether euthanasia is direct or indirect, says Professor Fletcher, voluntary or involuntary, is ethically something that depends on the facts in the situation, not on some absolute rule.

It must be understood that not every physician approves of orthothanasia. Some medical men still believe that they are obligated to do everything possible to keep life going as long as they are able. The patient might recover, they reason, suddenly and miraculously. They may find it impossible to tell when they are preserving life or prolonging dying. They feel that if it were definitely stated that a life need not be prolonged with every bit of scientific knowledge available, the door might be opened to abuses. What, for example, of the dying patient who wants to make a fight for it, but cannot communicate this, and is let go by those who feel the expense, and the anguish they are suffering, outweighs letting him live? Might not this be extended, once men feel they have no obligation to maintain life, to a patient who *can* communicate his desire to live on, but whose wishes are denied because of overriding economic and social reasons, or because of a selfish relative? The reasons against orthothanasia, some feel, are the same as those against euthanasia.

Physicians also are concerned about lawsuits. These may be brought against them by patients, or relatives of patients who have died, people who have been wronged or who feel they were wronged. Although no physician, at this writing, ever has been found guilty in court of causing death for humanitarian reasons, by refraining from treating a patient, the possibilities are there. Lawyers generally agree, however, that in cases where death is allowed to come naturally, it would be exceedingly difficult to make a murder charge stick because it would be nearly impossible to determine the cause of death, let alone prove intent.

Although patients are allowed to pass away because doctors do not take heroic measures to keep them alive, public notice of such a policy is not met with favorably. A case in point concerned a directive a few years ago, from the superintendent of a London hospital, telling the staff which patients were to be resuscitated and which would be allowed to die. The notice, pinned to a bulletin board, said: "The following patients are not to be resuscitated: very elderly, over 65 years old; malignant disease; chronic chest disease, chronic renal [kidney] disease." The notice reportedly ordered that patients in the listed categories would have a yellow card marked NTBR (not to be resuscitated) in their records. If such a patient's heart stopped — the classic definition of death not now necessarily valid — no attempt was to be made to revive him by open chest massage or electrical stimulation. Reaction to the directive — which was subsequently pulled down — ranged from approval to shock and horror. A spokesman for the Ministry of Health said that no harm was done in the sixteen months the notice was in effect, and the order never was put to the test. No patient should be excluded from consideration for resuscitation, the ministry said, because of age or diagnostic classification alone. A British Medical Association spokesman said his organization could not possibly approve of the existence of any such rule, adding that a decision would have to be made by the individual doctor "according to the individual circumstances of the case and not according to any blanket rule." However, Professor Glanville Williams of the Euthanasia Society said: "It is right not to take unusual measures to resuscitate patients when they are very old or suffering badly."

It cannot be emphasized too strongly that life is a precious commodity, not to be taken lightly. To take it thus would be to open a Pandora's box of wrong behavior and contribute to man's already well-known tendency to violence and destruction, in war and on our streets. The result would inevitably be a brutalized society. Every man has a right to life, and no one has license to dispose of it on a mere whim. What is being discussed in medical and moral circles today is not whether man has a right to life — but whether the dying have a right to die as peacefully as possible. This right may, in some cases, outweigh the right of the physician to try to extend that life by operations such as heart transplants, or long drawn-out resuscitative techniques.

"To sacrifice human dignity at the time of death," the dean of the University of Michigan Medical School, Dr. W. N. Hubbard, has said, "or to make the process of dying a burden upon the living, is not in the highest tradition of medicine, nor is it justified in the humanist traditions."

Five

Abortion

An abortion occurs when a fetus, or developing infant, is expelled or removed from the womb before it is able to live a separate life — usually when it is less than twenty-eight weeks old. The cause of much heated debate, abortion pits those who see termination of a pregnancy as sometimes desirable for medical, social or economic reasons against those who view the fetus as a human person and its deliberate destruction as murder. Physicians, theologians, lawyers and social scientists engage in arguments which grow in intensity each time a call is sounded for revision of state laws to make it easier for a woman to secure an abortion.

Abortion is not a new issue. It was practiced in many societies during all periods of history. Neither the Greeks nor the Romans had laws prohibiting it, and the ancient Incas of the South American Andes are known to have used powerful drugs to induce abortions. The practice of abortion down through the ages, however, was not always condoned. In Assyria, a strict moral code and written laws prohibited abortion and punished any woman attempting it with death. Judeans regarded abortion as a heathen practice and shunned it. In ancient Persia, abortion was the worst possible offense, carrying a death penalty. In India, it once was a crime equal in seriousness to the murder of a Brahman, a member of the highest, or priestly, caste among the Hindus. And the Oath of Hippocrates states, "I will not give to a woman an instrument to produce abortion."

Both in the United States and in Great Britain, abortions were tolerated so long as the fetus had not "quickened" — the term for the stirring of an infant in the womb, usually after sixteen to twenty weeks of pregnancy — until 1803. In that year, Britain's criminal laws were revamped and King George III signed an abortion law. In effect, this made it a crime for anyone to use a poison to bring on an abortion, before or following quickening. Later, the law set the pattern for others in the United States, and subsequently abortion before quickening was a crime in every state. In 1821, the nation's first abortion law was enacted by Connecticut. Other states took Connecticut's lead, but many allowed an abortion if necessary to save the mother's life.

In the meantime, abortion's most outspoken foe, the Roman Catholic Church, in 1869 adopted the attitude it holds to this day — that abortion is not justifiable for any reason, including a threat to the mother's life, and that it constitutes murder.

Laws governing abortion in Europe range from complete prohibition in Ireland and Belgium to abortion on request in Hungary and the Soviet Union. The predominantly Catholic countries of western and southern Europe have the most restrictive legislation.

In 1938, Great Britain passed a law permitting therapeutic abortions (those performed legally in a hospital) in pregnancies resulting from rape. A liberalized law permitting abortions if there was risk to the fetus or danger to the physical or mental health of the mother or any existing children of her family was passed in 1967. According to its backers, it considerably reduced the number of illegal abortions in that country.

In the United States, it has been estimated that around 1.2 million illegal abortions are performed every year, about a third of them by physicians. The rest are carried out by unlicensed practitioners working in rented rooms, dingy attics, garages and motels, or by the desperate women themselves. Thousands of mothers die each year because of these illegal and dangerous tactics. Other women have been forced to seek abortion in foreign countries. In 1962, Mrs. Sherri Finkbine, a television personality, went to Sweden to end a pregnancy after she found that a medication she had been taking, thalidomide, was responsible for thousands of deformed children being born to mothers who had taken the drug in the early weeks of pregnancy. An Arizona hospital had agreed to abort Mrs. Finkbine "on psychiatric grounds in the likelihood of fetal deformity," but the hospital finally backed down. In Sweden, doctors aborted her child, and found that it was deformed. In 1963, more pressure for liberalized laws was applied after a rubella (German measles) epidemic caused thirty thousand United States babies to be born defective.

As matters stand in the 1970's in the United States, most abortion laws permit an abortion in a hospital, but only if the woman's life is put in danger by her pregnancy. By 1970, twelve states had reformed their laws, permitting abortions for other reasons. These include the possible birth of a defective child, pregnancy resulting from rape or incest, or the probability of danger to the mother's physical or mental health. Among the states with the most lenient abortion laws today are Hawaii, which leaves abortion entirely to the discretion of a woman resident of the state and her physician, and New York, which has no residency requirement.

In 1970, the American Medical Association voted, for the first time in its 123-year history, to permit physicians to perform abortions for social and economic, as well as medical, reasons. The AMA's position required that the doctor performing the operation be properly licensed, that the operation be done in an accredited hospital, and that two other physicians be called in for consultation.

In varying degrees, proponents of a more liberal attitude toward abortion believe it to be the right of every woman, necessary if the physical or mental health of the mother is affected, or if the baby will be born defective, or simply if the child is unwanted for reasons ranging from a home situation in which another child would place a grave financial burden on the family to a mother's qualms about bringing a child into an imperfect world. It is not a matter to be decided by lawyers or clergymen, some feel, but by the woman alone, acting on the advice of her doctor. Like proponents of euthanasia, they place great emphasis on the quality of human life, reasoning that it is better not to bring a child into the world if it and/or its parents are to be reduced to a subhuman state because of the birth. Both scientifically and legally, the advocates say, the fetus is not a human being. It is not human because it cannot live without its mother, nor can it inherit an estate or sue for damages in a court of law. Its destruction might be considered an act of mercy, done both for the good of those directly concerned and for society. It also is regarded as a matter of self-defense, if the mother's life is at stake.

Opponents, notably the Catholic Church, see abortion in a different light. They view the destruction of a fetus as the end of a future, the obliteration of someone who might one day preside over a nation, develop a cure for cancer or win an Olympic Gold Medal. They maintain that the fetus is a human being, biologically and legally, and that its destruction, no matter for what purpose, is immoral. Their argument runs the same as that against euthanasia: that there is a law above mercy, that no one has a right to take a life, even though the motive is unselfish, that it is the duty of a physician to preserve life, using ordinary means, despite the possibility the life will be a defective one, and even if those responsible for it might suffer.

While some who oppose abortion might favor it in certain circumstances, they strongly denounce the most liberal pro-abortion position, which would permit abortion on demand, as a form of God-playing. Doing away with unwanted children simply at the request of the mother for personal convenience is as callous as runaway euthanasia, and to follow such a course would result in a weakening of society's moral fiber. Life's quality, of course, is important, but if the choice is between being born in dire poverty or not at all, of being malformed or not being given a chance, of being wanted or being destroyed — then the basic human right to be born and to live must win out. If not, say those against abortion, then life's quality is held in greater esteem than life itself. They cite the Constitution's Fourteenth Amendment which grants to human beings the right not to have life taken without due process of law. They express concern over the fact that the fetus can have no trial and that its destiny is decided only by mother and physician, with only the mother's rights being considered. And finally, they believe that one cannot be opposed to capital punishment, murder in the streets and the killing of defenseless civilians in wartime — as are most of those who favor abortion — and still be for abortion. In the final analysis, opponents see abortion as the intentional destruction of a human life for one purpose and one purpose only — to prevent the birth of a human person. The motive is not important, since life is God's greatest gift. And since it is innocent and defenseless, all the more reason for protecting it.

While the Catholic Church raises the strongest voice against abortion, many in its ranks, though they continue to oppose the procedure, feel it should be left up to individual conscience rather than be prohibited by law. Most members of the Protestant and Jewish faiths, on the other hand, recognize abortion under certain circumstances. Even among these groups, however, there are differences of opinion. A number of Jews, for example, feel that their race ought to realize that in allowing lives to be taken, say, to eliminate defective children, the reasoning is the same as that of Hitler when he sought extinction of the Jews because they were not on a par with the "master race."

A number of physicians also oppose abortion on grounds other than religious ones. Some believe that abortion is a social matter and that doctors ought not to become involved in the argument. Others hold there never are any reasons for an abortion, and that a woman with heart trouble or diabetes should survive pregnancy given proper and adequate medical care. Some emphasize treating the fetus as a patient and improving the environment he will be born into. And a number of psychiatrists are opposed because of the emotional injury an abortion might cause; it is argued that women risk serious depression after the operation because they really want to bear children.

Abortion, it is obvious, raises a number of questions. Central among them is whether the taking of fetal life is the same as killing a human being. Does the unborn child have legal rights to life, the same as a newborn babe? When, actually, does human life begin? Does it begin with conception, when sperm and egg unite, with the embryo that grows from that union, with the fetus that evolves from that? Or, since human life does not spring suddenly from a stick of wood or a stone, is it like a train on a stretch of railroad track that has been mapped out and laid down by a master engineer, with birth and death only stops along the way? Is human life traveling on a long journey through time, passing from cell to cell, organism to organism, with a common beginning somewhere in the misty past and a probable end somewhere in the faraway future? Or does life become human only when it can survive on its own, outside of its mother, when its environment, social and physical, can mold it and help it?

There are few black-and-white answers to the questions. Scientists and philosophers have asked them for centuries, and they presumably will be asking them long after the pages of this book yellow and fall to pieces, long after we and those who follow us pass on.

Science, however, does furnish us with some basic working material. And while science, particularly biology, may not answer all the above questions it can at least give us some clues and a foundation for discussing the abortion issue. But before examining these questions, a review of the reproductive process and a look at the world in which the unborn child lives might be useful.

A poet, who once asked in rhyme the question, "Where did you come from, baby, dear?" put these answering words into the mouth of a newborn child: "Out of the everywhere, into here." The answer is not too far from the truth when you stop and consider that a baby begins when a female egg cell, one of thousands that develop in the woman's ovaries, or sex glands, is fertilized by one and only one of the several hundred million male sperm in each individual. At this precise mo-

ment, the child's sex is determined, as well as his hereditary traits. The fertilized egg, called a zygote, now
carries forty-six chromosomes, twenty-three from the
mother and twenty-three from the father if the process
goes normally. These chromosomes are made up of thin
strands of a substance called DNA (short for deoxyribo-
nucleic acid), the genetic material which dictates every
individual's physical characteristics, from body build to
eye color. The egg now begins its slow journey down the
Fallopian tubes, ducts which connect the ovaries to the
womb. As it drifts, it divides in a process known as
mitosis. About a week after conception this mass of
cells, now about one-fiftieth of an inch in diameter,
attaches itself to the soft wall of the uterus, or womb.
There, growing and now resembling a tiny mulberry,
the mass arranges and rearranges itself, eventually form-
ing three layers out of which will develop the different
parts of the body — the skin, the digestive tract, the
skeleton and nervous system.

Up until it is three months old, the developing human
being generally is known as an embryo. After that it is
called a fetus. (Some refer to the embryo as a fetus after
five weeks, others after nine.)

In the early embryonic stages, of course, the unborn
child does not look at all like a human being. It grows
quickly, however, and in seven or eight weeks it becomes recognizable as a rudimentary person, although it
is only about an inch long. Its brain, at this point, has
developed enough to control its own simple movements,
its limbs have formed, its stomach, liver and kidneys are

functioning, and its heart has been pumping for some time. As it continues to grow — floating, like a tiny astronaut, in a fluid-filled sac called the amnion and fed by the mother through the umbilical cord which has kept it attached to the wall of the uterus since it was a "mulberry" — the fetus begins to show its sexual characteristics; it develops fingerprints, grows nails, swallows and sucks, grows hair, eyebrows and lashes. It "quickens" and lets its mother feel its presence in the fourth or fifth month. At six months, its growth has been astonishingly rapid. Now a foot or so long, were it to be born now, prematurely, it could live, in an incubator which simulates the environment of the womb. As the weeks go by, the infant's chances of surviving outside the womb are better. Somewhere around the thirtieth week, the fetus begins to assume a head-down position in the womb in preparation for its birth. Finally, expelled into the world by the pressure of its mother's labor roughly nine months after conception, the fetus is on its own. It weighs, on the average, about seven pounds, and is around twenty inches long. Interestingly, were the fetus's phenomenal growth during the second three months to continue without nature's check on it, at maturity it would cover the world.

Fetal existence probably is the most dangerous time of our lives. It is particularly hazardous during the first trimester (three-month period) when drugs taken by the mother, such as thalidomide, and diseases such as German measles, can cause deformity and mental retardation. There are other hazards, too. For example, some defect in the lining of the uterus may prevent the fertilized egg from attaching itself (estimates say this happens to one egg in three), and it is lost. Abnormal chromosomes, or the wrong number in the mix at the moment of conception, may be responsible for the birth of a defective child. This is the case in mongolism, when the chromosomes inherited by the fetus total forty-seven instead of forty-six. Research has been able to demonstrate that children born to women who smoked ten or more cigarettes a day when pregnant are slower readers and less well adjusted at age seven than children born of non-smoking mothers. Other scientists have shown that loud noise, such as the boom of an airplane breaking the sound barrier, may harm infants before birth. It has also been suggested that children born to mothers suffering from severe emotional strain during pregnancy cry more and have more stomach ailments than those born to other mothers.

Spontaneous abortion is a problem during the early months. This occurs when the fetus, unable to survive on its own, is expelled from the mother. It is also called a miscarriage. Some 5 to 15 per cent of all pregnancies end this way for a number of reasons, including abnormal development of the embryo, vitamin or hormone deficiency, infection or physical activity. Three out of four of these (it may be a zygote that aborts unnoticed, or the larger embyro) occur in the first trimester — the time before the embryo becomes a fetus. Serious maternal disorders such as pneumonia, typhoid fever and malnutrition may cause spontaneous abortion. Studies by Dr. Jack B. Bresler, a Tufts University scientist, have shown that national origin may influence fetal loss, with the number of spontaneous abortions and still-births increasing as the number of countries of birth in the grandparents' generation increases. It also has been found that fetal loss increases as the distance increases between the birthplaces of parents within the continental United States. Another statistical survey showed that at almost any stage of development, fetuses are at a greater risk of being expelled from the uterus during summer than winter months.

Spontaneous abortion should not be confused with premature birth, which takes place when a fetus, capable of life outside the mother, is set free before the full nine-month growth period is completed. A premature birth can occur six or seven months after conception, and is the most common cause of infant death in the United States, accounting for about half of all newborn mortality. A number of factors, such as disease, poor diet, or severe infection in the mother, may induce birth before term. Smoking has been implicated here also, with research suggesting that the incidence of premature births is twice as great in mothers who smoke during pregnancy. Any birth less than five and one-half pounds is regarded as premature, and the general rule has been that infants with low birth weights should not be discharged from a hospital until they reach that weight. (In 1936, a twelve-ounce baby was born at six months in Chicago, and survived to adulthood.) Incubators, which are artificial wombs, are credited with saving many premature babies.

But while the fetal period is a precarious time, doctors are able to keep a close watch on the little "astronaut." Science has developed special tools to enable the physician to peer into the fetus's dark and mysterious world. For instance, he uses ultrasound waves, inaudible to the human ear, to "hear" the fetus nestled inside its mother; by studying the different types of echo returned by different types of tissue, he can determine such things as fetal head size and brain temperature. He uses X ray and fluoroscopy to visualize the interior of the uterus, as well as miniature fiber-optic cameras and devices called endoscopes inserted through the cervix, the mouth of the womb. The fetologist, as the specialist concerned with the fetus is called, also employs another dramatic technique, amniocentesis. Small amounts of the infant's fluid environment are drawn off and the cells it contains — from the skin of the fetus or the amniotic membrane — are studied to determine fetal health or genetic damage. By studying this fetal fluid, the fetologist gets valuable clues about such things as chromosomal abnormalities, fetal age and sex, illnesses due to poisons absorbed from organisms in the system, maternal diabetes and Rh-disease, a blood disorder which can be treated by transfusing fresh blood into the fetus even as it lies in the uterus. Now one of the most exciting fields in medicine, fetology may, in the future, save the thousands of babies who would abort spontaneously, and enable surgeons to operate on malformed and diseased fetuses long before they are born. It might also mean — and the possibility is not all that remote — that scientists will manipulate and rearrange genes and chromosomes to correct birth defects at the time of conception.

Techniques such as amniocentesis, of course, also are valuable for the physician who has been called upon to decide whether to perform what is called a therapeutic abortion — to abort a woman for the health reasons cited earlier. It is because several diseases can now be detected quickly this way that many physicians feel they should be allowed to terminate a pregnancy that could come to grief — for itself as well as for the mother. Other physicians, as we have said, oppose abortion as the wrong approach, preferring to place more emphasis on treating the fetus as a patient. (The argument can be batted about like a tennis ball, for there are some physicians who feel that fetal manipulation, even for the good of the fetus, is playing God.)

Therapeutic abortions, those performed in a hospital for the various reasons cited earlier, are usually done before the twelfth week. (New York's law allows abortion through the sixth month of pregnancy.) Considered a safe and painless procedure when done by a specialist, it requires only brief hospitalization. Performing an abortion after three months obviously adds to the risk.

It is this "operative interference," the abortion that is performed deliberately, that raises the moral and scientific questions asked earlier about the fetus's status as a human being, and whether or not it has any rights. Exactly what is destroyed by an abortion? Human life or not? And if so, at what point did it become thus?

To understand the issues, we need to understand the distinction between life and human life. Life has existed on this planet for some time. Life, in fact, according to the scientific evidence, reaches back some 3.1 billion years. One explanation goes something like this: Our earth probably was condensed from dust some 4.5 billion years ago. Sometime after, violent forces, including electrical discharges such as lightning, produced amino acids in an atmosphere of methane, ammonia and water vapor. Amino acids are the building blocks of protein, an essential component of all living matter on earth. Nourished in the warm chemical "soup" that made up the early oceans covering the earth, a process of chemical evolution took place. The amino acids combined with others, and when the right combination was achieved, life began. (In 1953, experiments produced amino acids by electrical discharges in a mixture of hydrogen, ammonia, methane and water. Scientists believe that today the conditions are ripe on other planets, such as Jupiter, for life to arise spontaneously, from nonliving matter, as it did on the early earth.) Life, then, according to most biologists, is the result of natural physical and chemical reactions and processes.

Most theologians and a number of scientists as well believe that the essence of human life is a "soul" or "spirit" infused in the living organism by a divine being. This soul can exist apart from the body, and its life can continue after the death of the body. And scientists will, for the most part, acknowledge that there is no absolute evidence to either confirm or deny this.

Scientists generally agree that the moment the female egg cell is fertilized by the male sperm, the time of conception, marks the beginning of a new person's life. (Some scientists insist on muddying up a rather easy answer by stating that the new individual may actually begin developing with the selection of the twenty-three heredity-bearing chromosomes for the sperm and the twenty-three for the egg, or with the selection of the one sperm to fertilize the egg.) What really splits the pro-abortionist from his opponents is the question: Is the zygote, embryo or fetus an *actual* human being, with a soul, in the traditional sense?

In the view of the Catholic Church, life becomes human with a soul at conception. It is not, the Church holds, merely a growth or an appendage or a group of cells, but actually existing human life and not potential human life. This life — zygote, embryo and fetus — has the same rights as a born person. It is biologically separate from the mother and it has a right to be born and the right to all the know-how that medicine can muster to enable it to live as healthy a life as possible. Catholics are not alone in this opinion. The respected Protestant theologian Karl Barth said that the unborn child is a child from the very start, though still developing and with no independent life. "But it is a man," he wrote, "and not a thing, not a mere part of the mother's body. He who destroys germinating life kills a man." Another scholar, Professor Paul Ramsey of Princeton, found no difference between abortion and infanticide.

Others believe the fetus does not gain its soul until it has grown to the point where it can exist outside the mother's body. They argue that it is not possible for a rational soul which represents, or actually is, a human being to be present in a zygote or fetus because these are only potential, not actual, human beings. The soul is not the person — only the whole complex, the composite, the synthesis is. Put another way, this view of the soul holds that while it might be a substance in itself, when it finds itself separated from the body it is an incomplete substance. It is only when it is part of a rational, vital human being that it is complete. Saying that a human being gets his start at conception — though indeed he may be human in a biological sense — is not the same as saying that the product of conception, in its early, formative stages, is a human being in a functional, rational, actual, ethical or intellectual sense, say those who see no evil in abortion. What is destroyed in an abortion is a potential human being and not a real human being; it follows, then, that no human life is taken, and abortion is not immoral or evil.

Let's draw a rather simple analogy to illustrate the two attitudes toward prenatal (before birth) life.

Imagine you are watching a sculptor at work on a piece of marble. He is just beginning, and the hard stone before him is as yet shapeless, a lump without identity except in the sculptor's mind. He chips here and there with hammer and chisel, and after a few minutes leaves the room on an errand. You examine the stone, noting that it still has taken on no form and, except for a few nicks, it looks the same as it had when the sculptor began. Acting on some impulse, you lift the marble, carry it to an open window, and drop it to the street where it smashes into a dozen pieces. What you did would be considered foolish and malicious, and the sculptor, if he caught you, would probably be satisfied if you repaid him for the ruined marble. Probably nothing else would come of it.

But suppose you had come upon the sculptor after he had spent six months or a year of tedious work on the stone, and it had been transformed, under his skilled hands, into a lovely face. If you destroyed it then, chances are it would go quite hard with you and your deed would be branded criminal.

Some people view the fetus in much the same way as they see the sculptor's stone — with its value increasing as it progresses further away from its original state. They see no evil in bringing about the end of the fetus's existence, through abortion, because he has had so little *past* history of existence. They agree that the closer the fetus is to birth, the more one is treading on dangerous moral ground, that to do away with a fetus at a late stage of development, or a child at birth, is to destroy, let's say, the sculptor's work of art, and waste all the past effort. But in the early stages, when the life within the mother is without recognizable form, when it is unable to live alone without the mother's help, the fetus is held to be potential human life and not actual human life, and to destroy it then is not morally wrong.

To others, the smashing of the sculptor's stone, even in its formless beginning, is a criminal act and immoral. Who can know, they might ask, why the sculptor chose that particular stone for his work? Was it some special quality, texture or grain? Was it that the quarry from which it was chiseled yielded a particularly hard stone, able to withstand more of nature's hard knocks than stones of a lesser grade? Would this particular stone, once formed into a head, bring joy to someone, even if the sculptor himself rejected it? In short, the opponents of abortion place great store in the future of the individual. It is evil to destroy that future, and it is especially bad because God's will is thwarted. And with regard to the argument that a fetus is not human because it cannot survive without the mother, the opponents argue that even after birth the infant is dependent on the mother and others throughout early life who will feed it, guard it and clothe it.

Interestingly, the Catholic Church's doctrine of "immediate animation" — human life and soul at the moment of conception — did not come about until 1869. Prior to that (except for a three-year period from 1588 to 1591) abortion was a crime only if performed after animation — a point about which there was little agreement. Some felt animation occurred forty days after conception for a boy, and eighty days for a girl. St. Jerome (A.D. 340–420) believed that to take the life of a fetus before it developed human characteristics was not a serious sin. St. Thomas Aquinas (1225–1274) felt that human life was not present at all during the first weeks of pregnancy. (Within the Catholic Church today, a minority still adheres to St. Thomas's belief; other Catholics, while they oppose abortion themselves, feel it should be left up to the individual conscience, rather than prohibited by law.)

The legal status of the fetus also is tangled in opinion. Some lawyers maintain the fetus is a human being with fundamental human rights the same as those of a born child, claiming that the law recognizes it as such. Others say it is not, that it has no rights until it is born; and they argue as strongly that the courts back up their claim. The truth of the matter is that the courts have ruled both ways and, in the United States, the rights of a fetus differ from state to state. Here are a few examples: Justice Oliver Wendell Holmes, ruling in a Massachusetts case in 1884, refused to recognize the legal existence of a fetus. But in 1964, the Court of Appeals of Maryland, in a split decision, allowed an action for prenatal injury in which the "plaintiff" was born dead. The Connecticut Supreme Court has held that the representative of a stillborn child whose death was caused by injuries suffered while it was a viable fetus, may sue the one who did the wrong. Legal action, therefore, has been allowed for a person who never was born. On another tack, in 1970, the California Supreme Court ruled that a fetus cannot be considered a human being under the legal definition of murder, which is the unlawful killing of a human being with malice. The ruling came in the case of a man who beat his pregnant wife, causing the fetus to be born dead with a fractured skull. Although the killing of a fetus may be considered by some to be akin to murder, the court held, it is a matter for legislative determination. (The dissenting opinion contended that common law considered a quickened fetus a human being.) If abortion were murder, say proponents, abortionists would be punished for premeditated murder and they are not.

It is evident in a discussion of abortion that the problems are delicate ones involving scientific, moral and legal questions that may never be answered to everyone's satisfaction. In one way, the issue might be decided if the United States Supreme Court rules that women have the inherent right to obtain an abortion simply because they want to end their pregnancy. (In 1971, the high court upheld the District of Columbia's abortion law, which prohibits abortions except when necessary for the preservation of the mother's health, but avoided the broader issue.) Even so, this would not soothe those whose moral and religious convictions hold a human life to be inviolable. Nor would it appease the legal opponents of abortion who could argue forcefully that while such a ruling might give a constitutional right to a woman, it takes one away from an innocent human being who has no voice.

There are convincing arguments on both sides. No one can say with complete certainty that there is a higher law than man's that forbids such things as abortion, euthanasia and capital punishment. Nor can one say with the same certainty that there is not. About all one can do is affirm the right of all to speak, to listen to the opposing views, consider both society as a whole and the individual, and then make a decision based on one's own conscience.

Six

Capital Punishment

In the previous chapters, an attempt was made to shed some light on attitudes toward two forms of death resulting from a human act — euthanasia and abortion. We have seen that those who argue in their favor offer basically the same justification for their views: that the quality of life is more to be valued than its span in days, months or years, and that the effect a life has on family and society must be considered. Opponents of euthanasia and abortion also approach them in similar ways, basing their opposition on the sanctity of human life and on the belief that God alone should judge whether it should be terminated. Indeed, one might say that, generally, those who favor euthanasia favor abortion; those who oppose one oppose the other.

With respect to another method of ending life, capital punishment, the above formula does not appear to hold true. Ironically, many if not most of those who oppose abortion and euthanasia argue in favor of imposing the penalty of death for certain crimes, and the vast majority of those who argue for abortion and euthanasia argue against a penalty of death. We will examine the reasons for this seemingly inconsistent situation a bit later.

The death penalty is the harshest punishment that one man may impose on another. It has been inflicted on criminals from the earliest times, in various "humane" and "inhumane" ways and for a wide range of offenses. Today, where the death penalty is imposed for crimes such as murder, treason, espionage, sabotage, rape, kidnaping, armed robbery, arson and train-wrecking, the methods most commonly employed are hanging, lethal gas, the electric chair, the firing squad.

In ancient and medieval times, death was meted out for many more offenses, some of them trivial according to modern-day standards. In India, spreading false rumors, killing a cow and stealing a ruler's elephant were crimes punishable by death. Judeans imposed the extreme penalty for cursing, Babylonians for selling bad beer. In the Egypt of the Pharaohs, giving false testimony was punished by embalming the criminal alive. Witches were burned at the stake for the hexes they conjured up, and heretics died at the stake during the Middle Ages for their "dangerous ideas." Among those punished for his radical views was the Italian preacher and reformer Girolamo Savonarola (1452–1498), who spared not even the Pope in his denunciations and who, with his brothers Domenico and Silvestro, was strangled and then burned by the executioner. In colonial America, a dozen or more crimes, including adultery, were punishable by death, although Pennsylvania, under a code of laws set up by William Penn, inflicted the death penalty only for treason and murder.

The methods of execution employed in early days were as varied as the offenses. Often, the punishment had to fit the crime: In Babylonia, if a building fell on the owner the architect was killed; if the building fell on the owner's son, the architect's son had to die; in ancient India, any man who broke a dam had to be drowned near the same dam; and for stealing military weapons, the penalty was death by arrows. Some societies allowed the condemned man, if he happened to be a high-ranking official, to select his own method, or allowed him to kill himself. In the Orient, there were some particularly imaginative methods of doing away with an offender. A victim might be skinned alive, or smeared with honey and tied to a stake outdoors where insects and animals made short work of the unfortunate culprit. Or the criminal might be sewed into a sack with a poisonous snake. Stoning was common (the martyr St. Stephen was one such victim) and mass drownings were regular events during the French Revolution. Victims of the Persians were crucified, buried alive, crushed under heavy stones, smothered in hot ashes, and trampled by elephants. Poisoning was relatively common, and the classic example of its use was Socrates, who was forced to drink a cup of hemlock, a brew made from a poisonous herb which numbed the body before bringing on death. Beheading, universally performed, was regarded as an honorable and noble way to be executed in the Middle Ages, while hanging was a disgrace.

But while hanging might have been considered a lowly way to pay for one's crimes, it has probably been employed more than any other form of execution, and during the reign of Henry VIII in England, for instance, more than 65,000 hangings took place, all of them public spectacles. As late as 1818, Great Britain had 220 crimes punishable by hanging. In that year, 808 persons were executed, 645 of them for crimes other than murder. Hanging and shooting were routinely prescribed in the United States, within or without the law: hanging by lynch law was widespread in the days of the Old West for horse-stealing and murder, and not a few sheriffs were judge, jury and executioner. Hanging remains on the books in several states today, but the firing squad has become a thing of the past except in Utah, where a convicted person has his choice of that or the gallows.

One of the most celebrated methods of taking a criminal's life is the guillotine, a decapitating machine consisting of two upright posts along whose inside grooves a sharp-edged, heavy blade rises and falls at the end of a rope. The device, still in use in France today, was named after the French physician Joseph Guillotin (1783–1814) who, as a member of the National Assembly, suggested that beheading be adopted as a quick and painless method of capital punishment. A widely circulated story that the doctor died on the infamous machine is untrue; he survived the French Revolution, a period in which the guillotine was used extensively.

Despite the trend in later years to humane methods of executing, the garrote — an iron collar tightened around the condemned man's neck — was still in use in Spain after World War II; during the war, too, millions died of starvation, cremation and asphyxiation at the hands of the Nazis.

The electric chair and lethal gas chamber were relatively recent attempts to make death come a bit easier. The first man to hear the chilling words, "The sentence of the court is that a current of electricity be passed through your body until you are dead," was William Kemmler of Buffalo, New York, who on March 29, 1890, had hacked his mistress to death with an axe. On August 6 of that year, in New York's Auburn Prison, he died in the first electric chair ever constructed. Death, however, did not come easily to William Kemmler. After the initial charge of one thousand volts surged through his body and a doctor had pronounced him dead, the condemned man moaned. The executioner's hand flew to the signal button, calling for more power. This time, two thousand volts cut through the victim, but once again there was evidence of respiration; Kemmler was still not dead. Warden and witnesses panicked. The deadly current was applied a third time, and held steady for four long minutes until Kemmler's life left him. He was pronounced dead eleven minutes and seventeen seconds after he had walked into the room.

The Kemmler case, and several others like it, gave some cause to wonder whether the electric chair actually was more humane and less painful than the barbarous means of the past. Nicola Tesla, the electrical genius whose work made the death chair possible, was one who felt it was not. The current, he said, may touch only one of the brain's four parts so that the individual remains conscious and suffers a keen sense of agony. "For the sufferer, time stands still, and this excruciating torture seems to last an eternity," he said. That view was disputed by Robert Elliott, a famous executioner who officiated at nearly four hundred executions. The heavy voltage, he maintained, instantly shattered the nervous system and paralyzed the brain before pain could register. Medical experts, he added, contended that unconsciousness came in less than 1/240 of a second. Painless or painful, death by electrocution was adopted by twenty-four states and the District of Columbia, and the gas chamber by ten.

Movements to eliminate the death penalty have been underway in many countries over the years. In several, the efforts were successful. Norway abolished capital punishment in 1902, Sweden in 1921, Holland in 1870 (except for various military offenses) and Portugal in 1867. Ireland, stunned by the assassination of President Kennedy, wiped out the death penalty in 1964 except in cases involving the assassination of a head of state or a visiting leader. There is no death penalty in Italy and in several South American countries, and Switzerland prescribes it only for treason by members of the armed services. A number of countries which did abolish capital punishment made an exception after World War II in order to execute traitors and war criminals. The Soviet Union abolished the death penalty after the war, but reinstated it in 1950, executing by firing squad those convicted of treason, sabotage and banditry. A few years later it was stretched to include aggravated murder and economic crimes such as embezzlement. Great Britain, which had probably hanged more people for more different reasons than any other country in history, abolished the death penalty in 1965. Bolivia did away with it in 1966. In all, seventy-three countries have taken the capital punishment law off their books.

In the United States, forty-one states in 1970 still allowed the death penalty. Michigan was the first to abolish it, in 1847. Wisconsin dropped it in 1853, Maine in 1887, Minnesota in 1911, Alaska and Hawaii in 1957, Oregon in 1964, Iowa and West Virginia in 1965. Rhode Island abolished it in 1852, except for murder committed by a prisoner serving a life sentence. Other states which abolished it except in special circumstances were New York, Vermont, New Mexico and North Dakota.

In states where capital punishment remains in the statutes, it is not often applied. In 1963, according to the U.S. Bureau of Prisons, 21 persons were executed by civil authorities, the lowest number since 1930. Only the year before, 47 were put to death. But during the 1930's, a peak period of gangsterism, executions averaged 167 a year (there were 200 in 1935). From that time, the number declined steadily: in the Forties, the average was 128 a year; in the Fifties, 72 a year; in the Sixties, 42 a year up to 1964. There were 7 executions in 1965, 1 in 1966, and 2 in 1967. From that year through 1970, there were none. (In all, 3,859 persons, including 32 women, have been executed in the United States since 1930.)

Approximately 651 inmates (including 7 women) were waiting on Death Row in U.S. prisons in thirty-three states in 1971. That year, the Supreme Court, in a 6–3 decision, upheld the authority of juries to choose between life and death sentences. Still open is the challenge that the death penalty is "cruel and unusual punishment" barred by the Constitution. More than a hundred appeals, raising that issue, are pending before the court. It is felt by many that capital punishment, as a means of penalizing criminals, is in the twilight of its existence. Whether or not circumstances, changes in the attitudes of government leaders or pressure from the general public will reinstate it remains to be seen.

Let's look first at the arguments of those who would retain the death penalty. Their strongest debating point is that the fear of death prevents some people from committing crimes such as murder, and that the vision of the electric chair or the gallows is far more horrible than the iron bars of a prison behind which a man might spend the rest of his life. Police officials, including longtime FBI director J. Edgar Hoover, are the most vocal adherents of this view, but a number of clergymen of all faiths, some members of the legal profession and a large segment of the general public share it. For years they have argued that the homicide rate rises when there is no death penalty; that most prisoners are repeaters, in jail on at least a second conviction; that the death penalty is the only language that murderers and other criminals understand, and that the life of a murderer must be taken so that other lives may not be sacrificed. Supporters of the deterrent idea feel that capital punishment protects law enforcement officers and prison guards and that murderers, whether free to roam the streets after a life sentence has been reduced or allowed to live out their lives in prison, would not hesitate to commit murder again, reasoning they have little to lose. How many awful crimes, they ask, would have been committed were it not for the threat of capital punishment hanging overhead? Should not death be administered, if only to remind potential murderers of what can befall those who take life so lightly? If it is not a deterrent, then religion ought to quit preaching hellfire and damnation as a deterrent to sin. The sympathy of society, they reason, belongs to the families of the murder victims and not to the murderer.

"The instinct of self-preservation is so fundamental," said a minority report of a 1959 Massachusetts committee to study the abolition of capital punishment, "that the threat of death must have a powerful determining influence on the voluntary direction of human activity." The purpose of capital punishment, the report added, is to discourage by the most drastic means possible the wanton taking of the life of innocent human beings. Among those adhering to the minority view was Monsignor Thomas J. Riley, formerly rector and professor of moral theology at St. John's Archdiocesan Seminary in Boston, who, emphasizing that his opinions were personal ones on a disputed question and not the official Catholic position, said: "The supreme authority of this state has the right to inflict the death penalty when it can be shown to be a necessary means for protecting society against criminal attack which endangers its very foundations. Society has not yet reached the stage of moral development at which it would be prudent to remove a safeguard judged to be necessary by so many charged with the heavy responsibility of protecting life against criminal attack." It would be wrong, his report concluded, to consider capital punishment a violation of the laws of God.

Another argument for retention has it that the death penalty saves the public the expense of the thousands of dollars it costs to keep an offender in prison. The electric chair and other means of disposing of a condemned man are cheaper and quicker. Keeping a convict locked up in an unnatural environment for years, or on death row as he exhausts appeal after appeal for his life, only to die at the end anyway, is more inhumane than swift death at the hands of an executioner.

The majority of those who argue against abolition of capital punishment do not want it to be used carelessly. And, few today, if any, would favor the execution of criminals simply because they are misfits. Some question the mandatory death sentence certain crimes carry in certain states, but all feel that to say the death penalty should never be applied is totally unrealistic. A stern sense of justice demands it, they contend, and those who oppose the death penalty give aid and comfort and security to the criminal. The abolitionists are characterized as head-in-the-clouds philosophers who have convinced themselves that murderers cannot help what they do, are motivated by some pressure, are not, then, guilty of any evil, and therefore should not be killed. And if this be their reasoning, argue the advocates of capital punishment, no criminal should be punished —

be he burglar or bank robber or embezzler — for the same reason that some social, economic or mental reason forced him to do his deed. Advocates of the death penalty also see as hypocrisy the reintroduction of the death penalty in countries which abolished it, as did the European countries which executed traitors. Is the life of a traitor worth any less than that of a cold-blooded murderer who wipes out an entire family? And what of Fidel Castro's Cuba which did away with the death penalty for criminals, but carried out mass political executions?

To return to a question raised earlier: Why would someone who opposes abortion and euthanasia, arguing that human life is the property of God, be in favor of the supreme penalty? Part of the answer is based on the belief, cited earlier, that life may be taken — in a just war, in self-defense and in a legal execution — if, and only if, society is seriously threatened. Part of it lies in the very fact that life *is* sacred. The reasoning goes like this: The Book of Genesis tells us that, "Whosoever sheddeth man's blood, by man shall his blood be shed." This judgment was rendered because God made man in His own image; many Christian theologians say, therefore, that anyone who breaks the law against murder must pay with his own life *because* life is sacred. A murderer must get his just return; the wages of sin is death. Another line of explanation which serves to justify the death penalty — offered by Buddhists — is that a murderer facing death must realize that he has brought his fate on himself; when he is punished for his crime, he is not punished by a malicious judge but on account of his evil deed. Thus, there is no contradiction in saying, on one hand, that no injury must be done to a living being, and, on the other, that the guilty must be punished. Punishment purifies the soul, and once the murderer realizes it, "he will no longer lament his fate but rejoice in it."

On the other side of the argument, opponents of capital punishment offer a number of arguments to bolster their position. Opponents of capital punishment do not believe fear of the electric chair stops a person from killing any more effectively than life imprisonment. While law enforcement officials might believe it cuts the crime rate, criminologists, clergymen and sociologists do not. If the death penalty were a deterrent, say the abolitionists, then the states without it on the books should have a much higher murder rate than those retaining it. The statistics, they argue, show that this is not the case. In fact, some states with the lowest murder rates have no capital punishment. Wisconsin is often used as an example. Between 1941 and 1946, the state, which did away with capital punishment more than one hundred years ago, had an average annual rate of 1.5 murders per 100,000 population. Neighboring Illinois, with the death penalty, had a corresponding rate of 4.4. What the murder statistics show is that the murder rate is approximately the same in abolition states as in death-penalty states, proving, maintain the abolitionists, that the shadow of the executioner has little to do with murder or other serious crime.

In reply to the retentionists' belief that capital punishment protects police officers and prison guards, the conclusions of the noted criminologist Dr. Thorsten Sellin are worth noting. After a study of policemen who had been murdered over a twenty-five-year period in eleven capital punishment and six abolition states, Dr. Sellin found that the murder rate in death penalty states was 1.3 per 100,000 population, while it was 1.2 per 100,000 in cities in abolition states.

The idea that state-administered death stops crime also finds itself on shaky ground when one considers the following: The night after ten men were hanged in Pennsylvania in 1877 for murder and conspiracy, two of the witnesses at their trial were murdered, and inside of two weeks five of the prosecutors met the same fate. In Merrie Old England, as petty thieves were hanged in public in a carnival atmosphere for pickpocketing, other pickpockets were busy relieving the spectators of their valuables. In fact, of 167 thieves questioned before they were hanged, 164 admitted they had watched public executions for theft. In Massachusetts in the 1920's, two murders were committed within forty-eight hours of an electrocution. In 1961, Delaware restored the death penalty after three brutal murders were committed; ten days later a detective murdered his wife. Ironically, only a few weeks earlier, the policeman had told a minister, in strong terms, that the death penalty was "a real deterrent to murder." And there was the case of a man named Hespel who operated a guillotine for many years in French Guinea; Hespel, who should have known the price, eventually committed murder and went to the guillotine himself. Cases such as this are not uncommon; murders have even been committed the night before an execution in the very shadow of the jail. Former San Quentin Prison warden Clinton Duffy, who asked hundreds of prisoners — murderers, as well as robbers who used guns and were potential killers — if they thought about the death penalty before they committed their crimes, remarked: "I have not heard one person say he had ever thought of the death penalty prior to the commission of his crime."

The above cases point up, say the abolitionists, that murderers and criminals do not reason as other people do. Most crimes are committed under extreme emotional pressure, and many murderers have no foresight and no imagination. Killings often are committed in panic or blind rage, and the murderer is oblivious of the consequences. (We shall examine motivation for murder in the following chapter.)

Interestingly, it has also been suggested that capital punishment stimulates crime. There was the case of an Ohio man who killed his wife shortly after a neighbor had been executed for murder, a case of "suggestive influence." In 1929, Dr. Alfred Adler, a noted psychologist, theorized that capital punishment was a stimulant to crime because the more severe the punishment the more attraction there was to commit crime. "All criminals," he said, "are afflicted with an inferiority complex. They feel they are not strong enough to make a living by honest means so they try crooked methods." In the one execution in 1966, James French was electrocuted in Oklahoma State Prison for strangling a cellmate. He had been serving a life sentence for murder. Just before he walked the last mile, he told a psychiatrist that he had been upset when his first conviction did not draw him the death penalty and that he killed again so that the state would execute him.

Another argument against the death penalty is that the months and years condemned men spend on Death Row leave them spiritually and mentally scarred. Among the instances of lengthy delay between trial and execution was the celebrated case of Nicola Sacco and Bartolomeo Vanzetti, a shoe worker and a fish peddler respectively, arrested in 1920 for the murder of a pay-master and a guard at a shoe factory in Braintree, Massachusetts. Seven years elapsed before the two were sent to the electric chair. During that time appeals for a new trial were filed; another man confessed that he had participated in the Braintree crime and that neither Sacco nor Vanzetti was guilty; the governor of Massachusetts began a personal investigation and numerous stays of execution were won. In his last days, Vanzetti wrote, "Just think of it. They have persecuted us to death for seven long years. Now they feel positive that we will be executed on August 10, after midnight. And yet they transferred us here [in solitary confinement], just to deprive us, for a month, of a little fresh air and sunlight, of some visits; just to inflict upon us thirty days more of solitary confinement, at the hottest of the summer, in a low, smoky, dreadful place before they burn us to death. And this is enlightened America."

More recently, there was the case of Caryl Chessman. One of history's most publicized convicts, Chessman was convicted in 1948 of kidnaping, robbery and attempted rape and was sentenced to die. While on Death Row in San Quentin Prison, he surrounded himself with law books, became a self-taught legal expert, and acted as his own attorney. Lawyers and judges were amazed at his knowledge of the law and his wordy legal petitions. Eight times, Chessman was able to win postponements of execution, financing the long and desperate sparring match with the government by writing four books. Foreign newspapers began to criticize American justice for allowing a man to be confined on Death Row for so long, and the Vatican newspaper, *L'Osservatore Romano*, called it "slow agony." The Chessman case touched off a strong movement to abolish the death penalty, but in the end Chessman lost. After vowing that he would continue to plead his innocence in hell, Chessman died in the San Quentin gas chamber in 1960, twelve years after he entered Death Row. "Demanding that a culprit pay with his life for a crime is one thing," Father Daniel McAlister, former Catholic chaplain at San Quentin Prison, said, "Inflicting this additional punishment is something else."

The real possibility that innocent men will be sent to their deaths also weighs against the death penalty. Police Lieutenant Charles Becker of New York, who was electrocuted in 1916 along with four gangsters in connection with the murder of a gambler, was pointed out by Thomas Mott Osborne, former warden of Sing Sing Prison, as an example of an innocent man "murdered by the state." Becker, Osborne declared, might not have been the highest type of man and he may have had a hand in several unlawful deals, "but he was no murderer. I would stake my reputation he had no hand in the case and yet because he fell out with gangsters he was the victim." He said witnesses were marshaled by the underworld to testify against him and secure a conviction. "And then they sat back and smiled while he was put to death."

It probably was a case involving the hanging of a man later believed innocent which forced Rhode Island to abolish its death penalty. In 1843, a wealthy manufacturer named Amasa Sprague was done in with an axe. Police arrested John Gordon, who had come to Rhode Island from Ireland only six months earlier. They also arrested two of his brothers, William and Nicholas, as principal and accessory before the fact. The prosecution reasoned that Nicholas bore a grudge against Sprague and that John Gordon carried that grudge for his brother and murdered the manufacturer. The evidence was circumstantial. The murder weapon was never found. William Gordon was acquitted, but John was hanged even before the case against Nicholas was brought to trial. Later, Nicholas too was freed, even though he was believed behind the murder. A few years after the execution, the story that the state had killed an innocent man became readily accepted, along with the idea that influential relatives of the murdered man had forced the authorities into swiftly punishing the Irishman. John Gordon was hanged in 1845, and the death penalty in Rhode Island was abolished in 1852.

Another case of the wrong man being accused of crime occurred in Mississippi in 1894. Will Purvis, condemned to hang for murder, stood on the gallows before a large crowd, protesting his innocence as the hangman adjusted the noose around his neck. The trap was sprung, but as the victim fell the knot loosened and Purvis rolled unhurt on the ground. He stumbled to his feet and muttered "Let's get it over with." But the crowd, in an odd reaction for a hanging audience, protested. Purvis was returned to his cell, and later escaped with the help of his friends. He hid out until a new governor, who had pledged to commute his sentence to life in prison, assumed office. Purvis finally was pardoned, and in 1917, an elderly man confessed that he had committed the murder. The confession proved to be true, and three years later the state paid Purvis five thousand dollars in compensation for his ordeal.

To the retentionists' argument that execution is cheaper than life in prison, the abolitionists say it does not cost the state more to keep a prisoner behind bars for life since most lifers support themselves; they repay the cost of their keep by filling prison jobs for which the state would otherwise have to pay salaries.

There is also the argument that a criminal tried under one set of circumstances and in one court may be handed a death sentence, while another man, who might be as guilty, would not because the jury has been more lenient, because he has a better lawyer, or because he has more money and social status. Opponents of capital punishment charge also that the death penalty is most often imposed on those who are poor and friendless, or members of minority groups. "I have never seen a person of means go to the chair," wrote former Ohio Governor Michael V. DiSalle. It is the have-not who "becomes society's blood sacrifice."

The death penalty has been criticized as a barbaric rite, morally indefensible, that brutalizes society by cheapening life. Quakers, for instance, hold that the deliberate destruction of a human being is a moral evil because killing destroys that of God in the victim, and the killer violates his own divine potential. There are other arguments against state-ordered death. There is the view that capital punishment is used more for public vengeance, to appease the clamoring gods of society, than to secure public justice or to deter crime.

The very fact that an execution is so final raises other doubts about its value. For example, it can have no corrective value for the doer of the wrongful act. One punishes a child, not to take pleasure from him, but to show him the error of his ways and to put him back on the right path; one cannot rehabilitate a dead person. "The function of punishment," said the Greek philosopher Protagoras, "is to educate the people in what is right or just." An execution not only fails to educate the executed, it fails to educate the public in what is right because it upholds one form of premeditated murder and opposes another. This finality denies that a person can mend his ways, that human nature can change, that the criminal can become an ex-criminal who contributes to society or who gains back his self-respect and self-control. There is a good deal of evidence to show that even convicted murderers can turn out for the better after release from prison. As a matter of fact, of close to three hundred Ohio lifers who were returned to society between 1945 and 1965, only two were sent back to prison, one for assault and the other for robbery. Since the death penalty is so final, say the abolitionists, all those who play a part in ending a life — judges, lawyers, juries, witnesses — must be infallible; and because this is not possible, society has no right to execute. "I shall ask for the abolition of the penalty of death," said Thomas Jefferson, "until I have the infallibility of human judgment demonstrated to me."

Those who call for an end to capital punishment decry the emphasis that has been laid on the treatment of the criminal after his deed, arguing that the death chambers and the prison walls are symbols of defeat, just as taking the life of a patient considered incurable is looked upon as an admission of defeat. Too little attention, they feel, has been paid to the prevention of crime. The abnormal conditions, mental and social, that encourage criminal activities must be remedied, or at least studied and understood; it is the disease which must be eradicated, not the criminal, for he is only a symptom of it.

Some years ago, the warden at Rhode Island State

Prison, Harold V. Langlois, said that it was better to keep murderers alive so that what made them murder might be understood. "All too little is known about the motivations, drives and behavioristic characteristics of humans who commit crimes of murder," he said. "The presence of such persons under close careful intelligent supervision can well provide an invaluable source of information in terms of research into human behavior. Legalized destruction deprives us of this invaluable source material. The availability and proper utilization of the findings from such research would be of invaluable assistance to our medical and psychiatric professions. Death as a penalty for death in our society is an expression of complete and drastic desire to do away with a problem, not solve it."

Capital punishment, which is now in its decline, may leave us for good, or it may not, depending on the temper of the times and the attitudes of those who make our laws and hand out justice.

But wherever one stands on the matter, it is difficult to fault the words of one of the world's greatest criminal lawyers, Clarence Darrow, who, at the conclusion of a murder trial in 1924, pleaded: "Do I need to argue to Your Honor that cruelty only breeds cruelty, that hatred only causes hatred? That if there is any way to soften the human heart, which is hard enough at its best, if there is any way to kill evil and hatred and cruelty, it is through charity and love and understanding. I am pleading for the future; I am pleading for a time when hatred and cruelty will not control the hearts of men, when we can learn by reason and judgment and understanding and faith that all life is worth saving, and that mercy is the highest attribute of man."

Seven

Murder

"Violence is as American as cherry pie," black militant H. Rap Brown said a few years ago. For those who view the caustic remark with skepticism there are enough examples to make the doubter a believer. The headlines scream them at us every day, and they tell of a drifter who kills eight nurses in Chicago, of the assassinations of John and Robert Kennedy and Martin Luther King, of a young man raining death down on sixteen persons from a sniper's perch in a Texas town, of a hippie "family" charged with sadistic murders, of a "model" child who murders his father, mother and two sisters; of a socialite who stabs her lover and then kills herself; of killing on campuses torn by dissent, in back alleys and barricaded rooms in our troubled ghettoes; of a wild shoot-out that claims the lives of a California judge and the three convicts who kidnaped him; of gangland guns snuffing out a life in a New Jersey field, of military rifles doing the same thing in a tiny hamlet in southeast Asia.

We see murder, which is unlawful and willful killing, each day on television and in movies; we read of it in novels, in history books, in the Bible. Cruelty and violence are very much a part of life in America as elsewhere, and while not all of us approve of murder or would carry it out, there is little doubt that it holds our interest keenly. Few of us, unfortunately, are shocked by murder and other violent crimes any more, and we almost have a tendency to shrug them off as "the way things are." We become cool toward murder, and when another human being is forced to die before his time we utter a gasp or two of token horror and we soon forget it.

Violent death is everywhere. It has been man's strong-armed handmaiden down through the ages, ever since Cain slew Abel, and the lexicon that places each type of homicide neatly into its own slot is a long one: fratricide, matricide, patricide, filicide, genocide, infanticide, pedocide and neonaticide. In America, the homicide rate is shameful, considerably higher than that of other civilized countries. In 1967, more than 5,600 persons died of gunshot wounds in America as compared to fewer than 30 in Great Britain, less than 20 in France and fewer than 12 in Belgium. In 1968, there were 13,650 murders in the United States, a 13 per cent increase over 1967. Between 1960 and 1970, murder incidence increased nationally by 62 per cent, according to the FBI's Uniform Crime Reports. And in 1969, 86 law enforcement officers alone were "feloniously murdered," compared to the national average of 53 policeman killings per year in the 1960's.

There is little doubt that America is becoming increasingly violent. Murder, for instance, has become the leading cause of death of Negroes between the ages of fifteen and forty. A 1970 government study found that the violence rate among urban blacks appeared to be strikingly higher than that for whites, and that the blacks made up most of the victims. Blacks who live in cities, the study said, are arrested eight to twenty times more than whites for such crimes as homicide and aggravated assault.

Since 1900, Americans have killed more other Americans with guns (the most likely weapon in all murders) than have died in foreign countries in every war that America has fought. And when Americans aren't committing murder they're more than likely exposed to it in various ways: one recent study of some two hundred cartoons showed fifteen hundred acts of violence, including killings and assaults.

Why do people kill? What kind of people turn into murderers? Are people born aggressive and hostile, or do they learn such behavior? Are man's actions governed by his own free will, or are they something beyond his control? These are some of the difficult questions murder raises, and the answers are not found in any one science. Psychiatrists and psychologists, for example, might look at a murderer's childhood, seeking some early causative experience, or at his history of mental illness. Sociologists concentrate on the environment in which the murderer lives, possibly laying the blame for his aggressive actions on poverty and despair. Others, physiologists, neurosurgeons and geneticists, see various physical abnormalities — everything from extra chromosomes to brain defects — behind violence and murder.

What then, do we know of murder and murderers?

To begin with, the law recognizes several categories

of homicide. First-degree murder usually refers to deliberate, premeditated killing, a murder plot carefully laid out and carried to its cold-blooded conclusion. Popular opinion to the contrary, relatively few murders, aside from gangland slayings, are planned and executed coolly. Killers are more apt to commit second-degree murder, which is killing in the heat of passion and with intent, but without premeditation and deliberation. (There is also the common charge of manslaughter, not to be confused with murder; manslaughter is unlawful, negligent killing but without malice, such as might occur as the result of someone's reckless driving.) Generally, murders are angry, spur-of-the-moment acts by ordinary, law-abiding citizens who strike out only in moments of blind fury. Or they are committed by those with some deep subconscious compulsion to kill. It has been said, in fact, that murder is not in general a crime of the so-called criminal class but of nonprofessionals, our relatives and friends. "Average," "model" and "good" people kill often, and they do so out of anger, fear, jealousy, panic and on impulse. Everyone, according to psychologists, hides an impulse to kill but, fortunately, control mechanisms in most of us — regulators fashioned by both heredity and environment — prevent us from turning into a nation of killers.

Studies have shown that one out of every ten criminal homicides is the result of a romantic triangle or lovers' quarrel. Three out of ten occur within the family unit. One analysis of English criminal statistics for the period 1886–1905 found that 90 per cent of the murders were committed by men and that two-thirds of their victims were wives or sweethearts. Another survey found that of the 13,650 murders in 1968, 40 per cent were committed during arguments between acquaintances, and 30 per cent involved closer associations. Some 30 per cent of murders have been blamed on drink, quarrels and violent rage, and another 40 per cent on jealousy.

Most murderers are men (2,000 women were arrested for murder and manslaughter in 1968, compared to some 11,000 men), but this apparently is not simply because men are more violence-prone. Clyde's Bonnie Parker and murderous Ma Barker should dispel any idea that women are, by their very nature, less disposed to crime than men. It has been suggested, however, that women are not arrested or convicted nearly as often as men even though they commit some of the same offenses. (In 1939, FBI Director J. Edgar Hoover noted that while only 7 per cent of the criminals arrested the year before were women, "nevertheless an average group of 1,000 female criminals commit more murders, assaults, larcenies and drug violations than an average group of 1,000 male criminals.") Traditionally, the courts and police seem to have adopted a somewhat more lenient, chivalrous attitude toward women, and when prison sentences are imposed they often may be lighter. It is interesting to speculate what effect the drive for women's liberation will have on the statistics. As barriers against women are lowered, the "weaker sex" could become less secluded and less domestic, acquiring more responsibility and independence in their personal and working lives. Such a drastic role change might conceivably cause them to be affected by the same factors that drive men to violence and murder, and juries might be less inclined to be influenced by sex.

As noted earlier, social, mental and physical deficiencies have been studied in an attempt to learn what makes a murderer. Some scientists maintain that aggressive behavior is innate and inevitable, others say people act that way because they learn to or are forced to. Some say it is body build, the country of origin of the killer's parents, or IQ. Climate is blamed, along with seasons of the year. Some rely heavily on environment, others reject it, arguing that if it were the prime factor everyone living in dire poverty in a slum would be a killer. Others place a good deal of emphasis on brain damage or abnormal genes, and while they do not minimize the effects of poverty and unemployment, they feel these are obvious and easy reasons that may cover the real cause of violent behavior.

It would probably be a mistake to take one of these explanations and accept it as the answer to why people kill or commit violent acts. A person may be born with certain characteristics that make him potentially violent — a certain kind of body build or organic brain damage, for example — but in the final analysis it would appear to be a combination of factors and influences — social, biological and psychological — that mold the murderer. To say that one factor is responsible is to reject others that have proved to be implicated and this sets up the faulty premise that everyone under given circumstances will kill. With that word of caution, let's look at some of the possible reasons people commit murder.

One of the earliest attempts to explain criminal behavior scientifically was made by Franz Gall (1758–1828), a German physician who tried to link the lumps, bumps and general shape of a man's skull to violent tendencies. The "science" he pursued came to be known as phrenology, but it was soon discredited. Late in the nineteenth century, an Italian criminologist named Cesare Lombroso came up with the idea that criminals were born, not made later, and that they could be recognized by certain hereditary, physical signs. The typical criminal, according to his thesis, could be identified by a sloping forehead, pronounced earlobes (or a lack of them), a heavy, chinless jaw, apelike ridges over the eyes, and either a good deal of body hair or none at all. Lombroso's man of crime would be extremely sensitive, or nonsensitive, to pain. Later, his theory was disproved by Dr. Charles Goring, a British criminologist who made a comprehensive study of several thousand jailed criminals and ordinary citizens. His conclusion was that there was no such thing as a criminal type based on physical characteristics.

This might have been the end of the matter were it not for a Harvard professor of anthropology, Earnest A. Hooton, who published a study in 1939 supporting the old Lombroso theory. Over a twelve-year period, Hooton studied some fourteen thousand convicts and tried to show that criminals had various physical traits that distinguished them from noncriminals (such things as low foreheads, small ears and wide, or narrow, noses). There also was a link, Hooton said, between certain crimes and various racial and ethnic groups. For example, his studies showed Italian-Americans at the top of the list in first-degree murder, and native-born Italians first in second-degree murder. Teutonic groups also rated quite high in first-degree murder, with "Polish-Austrians" leading in assaults. Hooton did not say that a given race was particularly prone to commit crime. What he did suggest was that certain races have a natural tendency or preference for certain types of criminal action. There is no scientific evidence to support the contention that any nationality or racial group is more likely to commit crime.

With respect to Italians, it must be pointed out that the vast majority of murders laid to them over the years have been committed during times of extreme prejudice, when living and working conditions were intolerable, or by members of criminal organizations such as the Mafia, or Cosa Nostra. The majority of Italians are law-abiding citizens, with no higher rate of homicide than other groups; if they tended to react strongly in times of stress, heredity could be blamed only insofar as the tendency to have a short temper, to become emotional or to have a low boiling point may be inherited. Much of this holds true for Negro criminality. Given the adverse conditions under which many Negroes live in the United States, one should see quickly that environment, not heredity alone, plays a starring role in their high murder incidence. Murder becomes approved conduct among members (not all, it should be understood) of a group reared in an antisocial atmosphere in which hatred and lack of values and self-control blot out any feelings of sympathy and respect for each other, as well as for those they see as oppressors on the outside. Many who live in such an atmosphere might never murder if the conditions around them were changed and they were given time to adjust to a more normal existence.

Among more recent attempts to relate physical characteristics to crime, the work of Sheldon and Eleanor Glueck of Harvard is noteworthy. While they emphasized that a number of factors went into the making of a criminal, they did conclude that there was some connection between body build and delinquent behavior. In their studies of delinquent and nondelinquent youths, their home environments and their IQ's, they found that youths classified as *mesomorphic* (of medium height, energetic and well-proportioned) were more often found among the delinquents than those classed as *ectomorphic* (thinner, longer body build and not so energetic). What did these findings mean? Simply that the mesomorph raised in a harsh and deprived environment was likely to react violently, while the ectomorph might not, even though he wanted to. The results of the study did not mean that body build by itself created the criminal — only that a given kind of physique could be behind a violent or nonviolent response under certain conditions. In this regard, much as heredity plays a role in shaping a person's emotional outlook, heredity would be a factor. The potential for criminal behavior could be inherited, but not criminal behavior itself.

Today, a number of investigators hold to the idea that abnormalities of the brain — diseases or what might be referred to as "electrical storms" — are responsible for crimes of violence. And many of these scientists, neurologists and psychiatrists, are of the opinion that slum conditions, while they do contribute to violent behavior, do not adequately explain such behavior. They cite rioting in city ghettoes, noting that only small numbers of those who live there have participated, and of those, only a few have engaged in murderous assaults. If slum conditions alone were the cause of violence, they ask, why then are most of the inhabitants of those neighborhoods able to restrain themselves? In a report in the *Journal of the American Medical Association*, Vernon H. Mark, William H. Sweet and Frank Ervin, all doctors affiliated with the Massachusetts General Hospital, suggested that "the obviousness" of what goes on in an underprivileged neighborhood may have blinded us to other possible factors, including brain dysfunction, in the rioters who engaged in sniping and physical assault. They referred to French and South African medical reports that indicated abnormal brain waves occurred six to nine times more frequently in persons found guilty of murder than in the general population. (One English study found that only one out of eleven persons convicted of killing in self-defense had abnormal brain-wave patterns, but that they were detected in eleven of fifteen people who killed without apparent motive.)

Does this mean that murderers and those who commit violent acts short of murder might be detected in advance? The belief expressed has been that at least a third, and perhaps more, could be identified before they harmed innocent people.

Studies linking brain impairment to violent behavior focus on the brain because it is the single bodily organ vital to behavior, be it violent or peaceful. It does not merely sit there in our heads, efficiently ticking away, operating all by itself. The brain is strongly influenced by our environment, and particularly by what other people do and say. In an earlier chapter, we saw that each person's brain-wave pattern, the result of electrical current discharge, is as distinctive as his handwriting. When the electricity stops, the person dies. When it misfires, however, abnormal behavior may result. Erratic patterns of brain waves, "electrical storms" if you will, already have been associated with certain physical conditions such as epilepsy, a convulsive disorder. These storms often occur in the center of the brain's temporal lobe, the chief site of impulse control, when the patient suffers from the so-called unusual epilepsies. These often present themselves without outward signs, but are marked by strange behavior, trancelike states — and outbursts of violence.

Deeper in the brain is the limbus area, believed to be the core of man's brain early in evolution, a primitive system linked to emotions and one that controls different types of behavior. Some of the electrical storms that lead to violence, Dr. Ervin and Dr. Mark feel, may originate in the limbus. To demonstrate the part abnormal electrical storms play in violent behavior, they implanted electrodes in the brains of laboratory animals. By stimulating its brain with electrical impulses, they could make a cat, for example, attack anything in its way. Similar reactions can be produced in human subjects.

It is because of this ability to switch anger on and off, along with the findings of abnormal electrical brain activity in patients at the time of their outbursts, that scientists feel that electrical disorders of the brain may be at the bottom of much violent behavior. They also know that the way such brain dysfunction is expressed, when it precedes violence, shows a pattern. Such things as periodic wife- and child-beating and street brawling, fire-setting, violent activity after small alcohol intake, an unstable work record and frequent, serious automobile accidents — all of these are the cardinal symptoms in the violence syndrome. Again, a word of warning about looking for simple answers. Not all murderers or potential murderers will have this set of symptoms; it is felt, however, that they should serve as an early warning system when they are present, with or without other signs of brain damage. And, with environmental changes, drugs or surgery, many patients with the syndrome can be treated and controlled, if not fully cured. Fine doses of radio waves at frequencies high enough to destroy tiny pieces of brain tissue at the site of the "storms" have enabled surgeons, for example, to stop seizures, to relieve pain and to control certain mental disorders.

Other experimental studies of the physiological basis for violence have resulted in some startling findings. By manipulating the chemical climate of the brain, for instance, neuropsychologists at Purdue University have produced striking and measurable changes in the behavior of cats and monkeys. Sated animals have been made to eat ravenously, and fits of rage have been induced.

The pioneer in the field of electrical and chemical stimulation of the brain, Dr. José M. R. Delgado, professor of physiology at Yale University, demonstrated in 1954 that he could control psychological phenomena in individual cats, rats and monkeys. He was able to evoke or inhibit learning, conditioning, response, pain and pleasure. By applying ESB (electrical stimulation of the brain) in experiments with humans, he was able to soothe violent patients, relieve pain, and influence mental functions such as the thinking process, speech and memory. Dr. Delgado's most sensational attempt to control aggressive animal behavior came in a bullring. Standing directly in the path of a charging bull that had been fitted with brain electrodes, he was able to stop the animal dead in its tracks by radio. In 1970, he and his team were able to establish, for the first time, direct two-way radio communication between an animal's brain (that of a chimpanzee) and a computer. Dr. Delgado also found that in man, the manner in which violence is expressed may depend on the social setting. In one instance a patient, who appeared to be out of control after ESB, refused to attack her doctor. This indicated she was aware of, and respected, his rank.

Scientists also know that chemistry is important in human aggression, just as it is in the moods of man. Male hormone, for instance, can increase aggressive feelings in adolescents who have feelings of inferiority. (Hormones are regulating chemicals that originate in the glands and are carried to all parts of the body by the blood.) Several drugs can elevate a person's mood, while others can cause depression. These swings of mood seem to be associated with key chemicals inside our brains. Scientists believe that drugs which affect man's emotional state may have an effect on these chemicals, called biogenic amines. How this happens is not quite clear. But it is known that the mood-elevating drugs tend to speed up the activity of some of these biogenic amines, while the mood-depressing drugs slow them down. This would indicate that the amines have something to do with mood and emotional state. It is still too early to tell whether the amines are involved in violent behavior or in mental disorders that can cause such behavior, but it is an interesting avenue of inquiry. At Princeton University, scientists, using a drug known as carbachol, which imitates the action of a brain chemical believed related to the transmission of nerve impulses, have produced some interesting reactions. Twelve rats that normally never killed mice were injected with the drug in the brain area responsible for emotion. Every rat, it turned out, killed mice placed in its cage. The scientists noted that the carbachol-induced killing had the same appearance as natural killing — that is, the kill was made with a bite through the cervical part of the spinal cord — even though the animals had never killed before, nor had seen other rats kill. Reversing the process, the scientists injected the killer rats with a substance that blocks the action of the brain chemical mimicked by carbachol. They stalked the mice placed in their cages, sniffed them, but did not attack. An experiment like this raises the possibility that drugs may one day be used to treat human aggressors.

Another approach to learning more about the causes of violent behavior has to do with the chromosomes, those tiny particles which carry our genes. Sex is determined by two chromosomes designated X and Y. Normally, the female complement is XX, the male XY. But in one of every five hundred male births the complement is XXY rather than XY, with the error leaning toward femaleness. There is an error in the opposite direction, XYY, and the situation that results often is referred to as "supermaleness." Unusually tall and somewhat retarded, this individual is found once in every two thousand male adults; he may be more aggressive than normal males because of the extra bit of chemical information he carries.

Many scientists believe there is a definite link between the extra chromosome and emotional disturbance and criminal behavior. This, however, is disputed, particularly in the courts when a defense attorney has seized upon the abnormality in an effort to get his client acquitted. Recently, a California judge declared that the effect of the extra chromosome on human behavior had not been scientifically proved, and that it could not be used as a legal defense in the case of a six-foot, three-inch defendant who was accused of assault. During six weeks of testimony, the court heard from a number of geneticists, psychologists and psychiatrists, including a research team from the University of Southern California and Cedars-Sinai Medical Center. Following up on British findings that six-footers in prisons have a high incidence of the XYY syndrome, the team had tested two hundred men over six feet tall at a state hospital. Eight of them, including the defendant, had the extra Y chromosome. The defendant's attorney argued that his client was forced, because of the extra Y, to commit acts "in an insane state of mind." A psychiatrist, however, testified that the defendant had a personality and conduct pattern no different from many of the XY prisoners at the institution. In similar cases in Australia and France, both involving murder, the Australian XYY defendant was committed to a mental hospital and the Frenchman got a light sentence. Despite the controversy, it is likely that the XYY syndrome will figure in other cases in the future. If the theory is confirmed, the impact will be far-reaching indeed. Again, insofar as the extra chromosome is an inherited abnormality, one might speculate once more that the *potential* for criminal actions is inherited.

In the search for answers to why people murder, a good deal of attention also has been paid over the years to climate. It is true that weather can be blamed for much of what ails mankind, and there is little doubt that climatic changes have been influential in determining the growth and decay of civilizations. A nation's fate can rest on whether a battle is waged in good or bad weather, various diseases ebb and flow with the seasons, and even our brains find they function best at certain temperatures (between 30 and 40 degrees is one estimate). Man is delicately adjusted to the weather, but whether it — along with the rest of natural environment — is associated with murder is difficult to say. The French lawyer and philosopher Montesquieu (1689–1755) was one who tried to find such a connection. In his most famous work, *De l'Esprit des Lois* (*The Spirit of Laws*), in which he analyzed the relation between human and natural law, Montesquieu argued that criminal tendencies grew stronger the nearer one lived to the equator, and drunkenness the nearer the North and South poles. Others felt that crimes against the person, such as murder, occurred more often in warm parts of the world, while crimes against property such as theft were more frequent in colder climes. Still others attempted to prove that crime incidence rose and fell in relation to barometric pressure, temperature and humidity. Prince Peter Kropotkin (1842–1921), a Russian geographer (and anarchist), even worked out a ridiculous mathematical formula to forecast the number of murders in any month in any European country. The prediction could be made, the prince said, by multiplying the average temperature of the month by 7, adding in the average humidity and then multiplying again by 2.

More recently, a study conducted by the Veterans Administration Hospital in Houston and the Houston

Police Department attempted to discover if there was a connection between weather and suicide (which may be a form of murder, as we shall see in the following chapter). The study of 91 suicides and 400 suicide attempts was extended to include homicide because it was thought that murder might show a greater weather relationship. Murder, unlike suicide, is concentrated in the evening hours (8 P.M. to 2 A.M.). Furthermore, suicides tend to take place inside the buildings, most often in the home, while homicide typically occurs away from home, frequently outdoors, and thus is possibly more influenced by the state of the weather. Dr. Alex D. Pokorny, who conducted the study, found no significant weather relationship to murder or to suicide.

Today, criminologists shy away from a direct relationship between crime and weather as unscientific and an oversimplification. It is true that murders seem to hit peaks in summer in some places, probably because people are more apt to be thrown together physically during that season. Hot weather also makes some people irritable and prone to anger. Crimes against property also have tended to rise in the winter in certain areas mostly because the cost of living goes up in places where fuel and extra clothing are required. But too often climate is confused with geography, and the statistical evidence showing certain areas of the country to have higher homicide rates — nearly half the murders in the United States occur in the South — leads one into the easy theory that it is the climate of these locales that makes the murderer. It is more apt to be the living conditions in an area, attitudes and prejudices, the style of life of the inhabitants, whether an area is urban or rural, local attitudes toward illegal behavior such as vice and gambling, and whether the police are more or less corrupt.

An explanation of murderous conduct in terms of psychology and psychiatry is closely related to many of the things we have been discussing — genetics, environment, chemistry, physiology. While murder and violent behavior do spring from a variety of neuroses, psychoses and emotionally unstable and mentally deficient states, these conditions, in turn, had to result from inside and outside influences. And that is where heredity, poverty, electrical "storms" in the brain, extra chromosomes and brain chemicals come in. For just as viruses infect us with diseases of the body, so do the "viruses" of childhood crisis and frustration, a broken home, a twisted chromosome or a chemical imbalance infect the mind. The mental conditions described do not automatically make a man a killer, but they provide fertile ground that makes it easier for the seeds of violence to sprout.

Several mental disorders are involved in violent behavior. One that should be mentioned is schizophrenia. This strange affliction, sometimes known as a "split mind" or a "dual personality," is the most prevalent form of acute mental illness. It is responsible for half the patients in our mental hospitals. It usually hits people who have been relatively normal, and it may show up all of a sudden or slowly. And when it does strike, it may affect the sufferer for a few days, or a whole lifetime. Scientists still are arguing about whether it is caused by some organic defect, or a disturbing environment. The world the schizophrenic sees is an unreal one, viewed as though through a distorted glass. He sees objects and hears sounds and voices that are not really there. Time seems to stand still, or it moves at a snail's pace. As he pulls further and further from reality, he begins to hide in childhood dreams; he believes he is controlled by some spiritual force. Because his thoughts, his moods and his behavior change, his whole personality also changes. It is a terrifying world, so frightening, in fact, that the sufferer often is driven to suicide. Sometimes he commits murder, killing what he once loved, killing because a voice tells him to, or killing because he wants to do away with someone he believes is persecuting him.

The schizophrenic, however, probably is not responsible for nearly as many crimes as the so-called sociopath, or psychopath. This individual is totally irresponsible, totally selfish. He lies, he cheats, he rebels against discipline and authority. Loyalty and love, sympathy and shame are foreign to his immature mind. Turned off, fouled up and put down, he lives in a gray world, "a little too crazy for prison, a little too sane for the state hospital," as one psychiatrist has put it. The sociopath can be a man like Adolf Hitler, or a gunman who murders for hire, or a "mad-dog" killer on a rampage.

But whatever the explanation for violent behavior — whether it results from environmental, biological or physiological influences or a combination of factors — sooner or later one must face the question of responsibility. Did the murderer know what he was doing? Did he know right from wrong? Was he sane or insane? Determining responsibility is a problem that has been debated for years, and there have been several attempts to resolve it. On one side of the argument are those behavioral scientists who cannot accept the idea of free will — the notion that man moves freely through life, choosing between what is right and what is wrong. Rather, they tend to see human conduct as determined by such influences as biology, society, emotions, culture and uncontrollable instincts. They reason that the criminal is not responsible for his actions, that he should not be considered a criminal by the law but a patient in need of psychiatric care. "Yes, he did it," they say, "but he could not help it." Even though he may be entirely sane, he may still not be responsible. This view condemns the crime, the murder, as immoral, not the murderer. It is one that is heard more and more today in religious discussions of sin and sinner, in which the evil is condemned and not the doer of that evil.

The law, on the other hand, has looked at it differently. Generally speaking, all our laws are based on the idea that man, with an intelligence that separates him from the animal, is responsible for what he does. This is so, the law says, unless it is proved that the offender is not responsible because of some mental defect. In 1843, the McNaghten rule (named after a murderer who was acquitted because he was judged insane) came into being, and was widely followed for years. Under McNaghten, a jury was required only to consider whether the defendant knew the difference between right and wrong. If he did not, he was ruled legally insane. The pitfall in this was that a jury was apt to rely on popular beliefs and prejudices about insanity, neglecting the testimony of experts in psychology. Later, in 1954, the Durham rule was drafted. This broadened the concept of insanity as a defense by stating that the criminal was not responsible if his unlawful act was the product of mental disease or mental defect. Under Durham, the court's use of expert witnesses was expanded. Nevertheless, determining a clear standard for responsibility still remains a problem, if only because psychiatrists often give conflicting testimony in court. Then, too, there is the murderer who might be ruled sane but who does not fit into any particular psychological or biological category; he might kill because of some reasons not yet understood but which do not express themselves.

Recently, Judge David L. Bazelon of the United States Circuit Court of Appeals for the District of Columbia wrote that possibly psychiatry and the other social and behavioral sciences might not be able to provide enough data to make a determination of criminal responsibility. "If so," he said, "we may be forced to eliminate the insanity defense altogether."

Eight
Suicide

The man who kills a man kills a man.
The man who kills himself kills all men.
As far as he is concerned, he wipes out the world.

These words, by the English essayist, novelist and poet G. K. Chesterton, express the seriousness of suicide. They suggest to us that no man ought to reject the great gift of life that has been bestowed.

Yet every year in the United States, some twenty-two thousand persons kill themselves, and another two hundred thousand or so try it. Suicide is a grave social problem, here and abroad, and ranks as the tenth leading cause of death in this country. It ranks third in the fifteen-to-nineteen age group, and is the second most frequent cause of death among college students. The rate rises sharply with advancing age. Persons over sixty-five, who make up one-tenth of the population, account for a fourth of all suicides in the United States. The highest risk group is made up of elderly white males (fewer blacks than whites, though in recent years there has been an increase in black suicides, who have a suicide rate four times higher than the overall national rate. The suicide rate for men is about three times higher than for women, but statistics show that women make three times as many attempts as men. On a worldwide basis, it is estimated that about a half-million people a year take their own lives, with the United States ranking near the middle in its rate of about 11 per 100,000 population. (Nations with higher incidences of suicide include Denmark, Sweden, Austria, Finland, Germany and Japan.)

Firearms, according to a U.S. Public Health Service study of suicide statistics for the period 1950 to 1964, are more frequently used than any other means, accounting for 48 per cent of all suicides in 1964. Hanging was second, accounting for 15 per cent of the total suicides. About 12 per cent were from poisoning. The only other category which accounted for more than 10 per cent of the suicides in 1964 was "poisoning by other gases." Of these, nine out of ten involved motor vehicle exhaust gas. Suicides, the study found, are more numerous in the spring than in any other season. The winter months appeared to be the months with the lowest number of suicides: a rate of 46 per day for December, compared to 54 per day for April.

Suicide has occurred from the earliest times. The Bible mentions a number of instances: Samson destroyed himself along with the Philistines by pulling down a temple; Saul fell on his sword, Ahithophel and Judas hanged themselves, and Zimri burned himself. We read of Jews who committed collective suicide rather than denounce their faith to satisfy the invading Crusaders. In ancient days, virgins killed themselves to preserve their virtue, and some religious sects prescribed suicide to ward off the pollution of sin. Hara-kiri, ceremonial suicide for those disgraced, was formerly practiced by aristocrats and warriors of Japan. And during World War II, we learned of the kamikaze pilots who dove their explosives-laden planes into American ships, giving their lives for their cause.

While some societies and religions have tolerated or looked with favor on suicide, it generally is regarded with repulsion. St. Augustine regarded it as a sin, and a number of Church councils refused to allow the corpse religious rites. Jewish law and the Koran, the sacred text of Islam, denounced it (the Koran views it as a more serious crime than murder). Medieval law decreed that a suicide's property be confiscated, and the body be dragged by the heels through the streets, face downward, or buried at a crossroads with a stake through its heart. In Dante's *Inferno*, we find suicides in the Seventh Circle, transformed into trees, and Harpies, ravenous monsters with women's heads and birds' bodies, feeding on the leaves, as the unfortunates cry out, "Like other spirits, we shall seek our flesh, but none of us may put it on again, for none deserves what he has cast away." On the other hand, Seneca, the Roman philosopher, reasoned that one need not be unhappy unless one wanted to, and advised, "It is in your power to return from whence you came."

With respect to the law, most states do not regard suicide or attempted suicide as crimes; some view suicide as a crime but not a punishable one, and attempted suicide as either a misdemeanor or a felony; but in the majority of the states, assisting a suicide is a crime, either murder or first-degree manslaughter.

Suicide

Why do people kill themselves or attempt to do it?

Again, as we said in the previous chapter on murder, the causes can be social, psychological, biological or a combination of factors. Indeed, murder and suicide may arise from a common root, and suicide may be termed murder's blood brother. Suicide is often a form of murder in which the desire to kill is turned on the self; the suicide does not want to die so much as he wants to kill. He may want to kill someone who has frustrated him and, through some conversion process, he turns the urge to kill back on himself; he kills himself — the hated object — to satisfy both the desire to commit murder, and to wipe out the guilt he feels for wanting to kill in the first place. Murder, on the other hand, may be a form of suicide in that the victim may represent the murderer in his subconscious mind. Some murderers may kill so that they will be apprehended and put to death — a form of suicide. Some suicides may provoke someone to kill them; by encouraging another to take their lives, they commit suicide.

It has been suggested that some black revolutionaries are suicidally motivated. Writing in *Psychology Today*, Dr. Richard H. Seiden of the University of California, Berkeley, theorized that many of these angry men literally seem to want to be killed by police. "It is possible, if not likely, that young black revolutionaries are at least partially motivated by a wish to be martyred, to be ceremoniously executed, to be destroyed in violent confrontation in which they may momentarily respect themselves and from which they will gain posthumous stature, regardless of what political or public-relations value their deaths may have," according to Dr. Seiden. Whereas conventional forms of suicide such as drug overdose are regarded as "soft" and "unmasculine" by young black males, "in the ghetto subculture, masculinity and courage are frequently defined in physical terms, and young black men assign a high value in being tough." Thus, frontier-style shoot-outs represent a "swift, uncomplicated, and more or less equitable means of resolving conflict" in their minds.

Studies have shown that many suicides are obviously homicidal. One study, in Los Angeles, found that 2 per cent of suicides are preceded by murders; and another study, of murders in England and Wales, showed that a third of them were followed by suicides. Further evidence that suicide may at times be a substitute for murder may be found in the fact that suicides tend to increase where murder incidence is low. Urban Negroes, as noted earlier, are arrested some eight to twenty times more often than whites for such crimes as murder and aggravated assault, but their suicide rate is lower. Some states which have a high murder rate have a low suicide rate, and vice versa.

But bear in mind that there is not one explanation for suicide but many. People who come from higher rungs on the ladder of success appear to kill themselves more frequently than those on the bottom rungs. Suicides, it is said, account for 26 per cent of physician deaths in the under-forty age group compared to 9 per cent for white males of the same age. The pressures of a doctor's life are believed to play a part in the higher suicide rate. There are geographical factors: more people living in Scandinavian countries commit suicide than those living in the Mediterranean areas. Seasonal differences have been noted. Religion enters the picture. The suicide rate in Catholic countries like Ireland is much lower than among Protestants and Jews. Urban suicide rates are higher than those in the country. Social problems often cause an increase in suicides. This occurred among the young in Germany after World War I, and among the Jews during times of persecution, such as during the Crusades and the Nazi period. In prisons, self-destruction is often seen by inmates as the only way out. Loss of a job can make a person attempt suicide; or ill health, or the death of a loved one, or a past attitude toward death which sees it as a blessing, a deep and troubleless sleep, or as a way to paradise.

But whatever makes the suicide pull the trigger — a wish for death, an urge to kill or a desire to escape from life — it is true that a great many are depressed, and face a personal crisis. The person who thinks seriously of ending his own life is drowning in a sea of problems, and he sees death as a relief. He is not concerned that he will be responsible for causing grief among his survivors, because something inside him has given way, and his own problems wash out any other thought. One study of one hundred young adults from New York's Upper East Side who had attempted suicide found that each was suffering from some form of psychiatric illness, with depressive features chief among them. The most frequently given reason for the attempt was hopelessness brought on by a threatened or actual loss of an important person in their lives. Some of the group blamed their attempts on alcohol and drug abuse; others, aware of psychiatric symptoms, became hopeless because they had isolated themselves. Another study of young suicide-attempt patients at Los Angeles County General Hospital painted this disturbing portrait: 20 per cent had a parent who attempted suicide, 50 per cent had a parent, relative or close friend who had tried to take his own life; 58 per cent had a parent who was married more than once, 62 per cent had both parents working, 74 per cent viewed their family conflict as extreme, 36 per cent were involved in the end stages of a romance, 22 per cent of all attempters were pregnant or believed themselves to be so, 36 per cent were not enrolled in school at the time, and 100 per cent of those in the end stages of a romance had had a serious argument with the partner immediately before the attempt.

Whether the suicide victim is sane or insane or temporarily insane when he does away with himself depends on one's view of what is sane and insane. If insanity is an emotionally confused frame of mind, or an inner instability that forces the person up against the wall under stress, then many suicides are insane. There are, however, many kinds of mental disorder, and it is hard to use words like sane and insane and be sure. Quite a number of inmates of mental hospitals, people who have been diagnosed as hopelessly insane, and many seriously troubled people under psychiatric care, never try to commit suicide. But, as in cases of murder, many apparently well-adjusted people have taken their own lives. The potential for suicide is in all of us; whether it comes to the surface depends on how well our built-in system of checks and balances works.

According to two University of Michigan psychiatrists, suicidal people act according to patterns set in infancy. In a report to the American Academy of Psychoanalysis, Dr. Edgar Draper and Dr. Philip Margolis said the "suicidogenic seed" is sown during a critical period when a child is between six and eighteen months old. During that period an infant becomes highly sensitive to his mother's responses to him. She becomes his first psychologically needed person. If she doesn't or can't respond to her child's emotional requests at this special developmental point, the infant suffers deep psychological pain. The doctors said this pain can surface in adulthood as a suicidal impulse, triggered by the loss of another psychologically needed person. The infant who is not physically or emotionally abandoned at the critical stage "is theoretically safeguarded against suicide."

It is not true that there is no way out, as many suicide attempters believe. The way usually is there, but the individual does not see it, or he is not able, or allowed, to take advantage of it. Alcohol, drugs, the tremendous pressure to conform, lack of purpose, or not being loved and wanted — all these may cloud the view of the person who seeks death. Some find the solution, others give up.

Suicide attempts are a cry for help, in the view of

many doctors, and each of these attempts must be taken seriously. It is wrong to believe that people who talk about suicide never do anything about it. Most people who kill themselves give some signal, some clue, before they do it because they want to be discovered and saved. They might make some statement as "I've just straightened out the will, so you'll not have to worry," or they might visit the doctor's office. One study found that about a third of suicide victims saw a physician on the day they killed themselves, and that three-fourths saw the doctor within four months of the time they did it. These presuicidal patients who appear in physicians' offices, according to Dr. Herbert O. Modlin, director of preventive psychiatry at the Menninger Foundation, actually are making indirect appeals for help. Most often they complain of some bodily ailment, but if the doctor asks the right questions they will reveal their real suffering.

It is also known that 12 to 15 per cent of those who succeed in killing themselves leave suicide notes. This last gesture may be a cry for help, or it may be the equivalent of a will.

Dr. John Altrocchi, a Duke University psychologist, says that under 10 per cent of suicide victims are psychotic (insane), but that half of them have a significant amount of alcohol in them at the time. "They have a feeling of self-condemnation and do not go directly for help when in fact they subconsciously want help. They often feel, 'I am not worth saving.'" A case in point might be the young University of Florida student who

tripped out on drugs and wrote, before he burned himself to death, "I have killed myself because I can no
longer run my own affairs, and I can only be trouble to
those who love and care for me. Please forgive me, parents, for quitting after you raised me, but I cannot live
with myself any longer. You were good parents, and I
love you both. Don't let my downfall be yours. You have
nothing to be ashamed of. I made the mistake, not you.
There is nothing but misery for all of us should I allow
myself to deteriorate further."

The method a person chooses to end his life is a clue
to the degree of intent. Taking pills or slashing a wrist is
not as serious as using a gun or jumping from a building.
"When a man contemplates suicide with a gun," says Dr.
Altrocchi, "he is more likely to succeed simply because
there is zero time to reconsider after he pulls the trigger.
Women who take a number of pills may have hours to
contemplate their deed and in many instances they do
reconsider and summon help." In the East Side study,
most of the young suicide-attempters chose poison, a
signal that their unconscious wish was to be found and
rescued. In the Public Health Service study cited earlier, it was found that a greater percentage of females
than males drowned themselves. While firearms accounted for 56 per cent of all suicides for males, they
were responsible for only 25 per cent of the female
deaths. Methods differ according to color as well as sex.
A greater percentage of white than nonwhite persons
poisoned themselves with pills and exhaust gas, the Public Health Service study found. Conversely, nonwhite

persons were more likely than white persons to use solid and liquid substances such as rat poison, lye and denatured alcohol, and to kill themselves by jumping from high places.

One interesting aspect of suicides is the suspicion that many accidental deaths — such as those that result from "chicken" games in automobiles or from one-car, one-occupant accidents — are not accidents at all, but suicides in disguise. They have been termed autocides. Dr. John Edland, chief medical examiner for Monroe County, New York, has said that 10 to 15 per cent of single-vehicle crashes are suicides. However, suicide by accident is hard to prove, and there is enough social pressure to prevent these deaths from being officially listed as suicides. (Suicide has long been a taboo subject, and many cases are kept secret by families and physicians because of the stigma attached to self-destruction. In these cases, a death certificate is filled out, giving only a medically acceptable cause of death.)

Studies of fatal illness suggest that psychological factors may be responsible for bringing on the so-called terminal phase. This is a period of no return at or near the end of life. One study, Project Omega of the Massachusetts General Hospital, has uncovered many similarities between those who give in to a fatal disease and those who give in to suicidal thoughts. Besides alienation from a loved one, these include despair, self-destructive tendencies, acute loss of self-esteem, refusal of help and the acceptance of death as the only answer to the problems of life. "We have found," says Dr. Avery

Weisman, the principal investigator and a noted authority on suicide and terminal illness, "that there comes a point in any terminal illness when a person comes to accept death as appropriate for himself and to yield to the terminal process. In some sense, this is what the suicidal person does. When that happens, there is the same kind of alienation from other people, of repudiation of help, of despair."

Suicides can be prevented, but not in the same way that disease can be prevented — by vaccinations and antibiotics and X rays. The problem is a social one, and not merely a medical responsibility. And so long as physicians shy away from discussing it openly with their patients, and the public avoids mentioning it except in hushed whispers, the problem will not be solved. Our attitudes toward death — enveloped in fear, shrouded in mystery and oriented toward a life we have fooled ourselves into believing will go on forever — must change. Because we see death only as inevitable, we close the door on learning more about it, and lives that could be saved or prolonged are lost. The person who threatens to take his life needs meaningful contact with others. He has removed himself from the mainstream, and he needs people who care, people he can talk to; he needs self-confidence. He needs a substitute for drugs or alcohol, the two trip-tickets to nowhere he has bought. He needs to learn about himself as he lives a complete life, that he cannot jam it all in with one pill. "It could be too much for your mind to handle at one time," wrote the Florida youth who chose not to be. "It could blow out all the circuits as it did with me." The suicide-prone individual must be encouraged to seek help from psychiatrists, ministers and at the many suicide prevention centers scattered across the country that provide twenty-four-hour emergency counseling. Too often, a visit to a psychiatrist is taken to mean that the visitor is "crazy." One does not hesitate to see a specialist when a bone is broken; one should not hesitate when emotions are involved.

As our fearful attitudes toward death — particularly murder and suicide — often prevent us from learning more about it, so too can a fear of life pose a problem. "As long as there is more dread of life than fear of death," writes the distinguished psychiatrist Dr. Joost A. M. Meerloo, "death will tempt people with the promise of greater security than they can find in this lifetime — unless and until such time as we are able to teach man to accept and embrace his own destiny."

Nine

Quest for Immortality

From the moment we are conceived, we age. The process, moving us slowly to the end of our allotted Biblical threescore and ten — unless disease, accident or enemy interrupts — is hardly noticeable from day to day. But on it goes as the biological clock in our bodies relentlessly ticks away the hours. When it runs out, we die. And nothing thus far has been able to reverse the process.

Yet man continues to search for eternal youth and life, or for something that will slow the clock if not stop it completely. Some, seeking a chemical fountain of youth, expect that man's life-span here on earth will one day be prolonged through laboratory science. Others, putting their trust in techniques involving preservation of the body, believe human beings will have life in some future age after being revived. Still others, putting their faith in one religion or another, see man living a life of eternity either here on earth — his soul flitting from one animal or human body to another — or in a place that is not of this world.

Whether it is the Buddhists' Nirvana, the ancient Greeks' Hades or the Christians' heaven and hell, the dream of immortality has been with us from the dawn of history.

But man's life on earth, unfortunately, is limited. How

long we live is governed by many things — health, diet, environment, heredity, the daily pace of our lives. When he first began to record history, man could expect to live less than twenty years. Today, helped along by improved medical care, better sanitation and proper nutrition, the life expectancy is around seventy.

Each day on this earth, some 140,000 persons die. Some 860 people die of cancer every day in the United States, more than one every two minutes. Nearly a million die each year of cardiovascular disease, 66,000 of high blood pressure. Hardening of the arteries, or atherosclerosis, is responsible for nearly half of all the deaths in this country each year. Infectious disease such as flu, pneumonia, tuberculosis, kidney infection, bronchitis and syphilis take 100,000 lives annually. Automobile accidents killed 56,400 in 1969. Some 30,000 deaths occur each year in housing-related accidents. We have seen the statistics on murder and suicide.

Barring accident and ill health, how long can man expect to live? The American male does not seem to fare as well as men in other countries. His life expectancy at birth is about 66.70, placing him twenty-sixth on the world's longevity scale. American females, on the other hand, live longer — to an average of 74.00, which ranks them twelfth in the world. Males who live longer than their American counterparts are the Swedes, with an average age of 71.60; Norwegians, 71.32; the Dutch, 71.10; Israelis, 70.52; the Danes, 70.30. In Iceland, females can expect to live to be 76.2; in the Netherlands, 75.90; in Sweden, 75.70; in France, 75.10; in Russia,

74.00. Sweden boasts the lowest death rate for infants — 12.9 per 1,000 live births. The United States rate, 21.7 per 1,000, ranks number thirteen in infant mortality. It has also been estimated that between 10,000 and 15,000 American babies die each year of unexplained causes.

While it has not been proved conclusively that diet affects the death rate, most scientists agree that the American eating habits — heavy on fats and rich foods — are a factor in the relatively poor showing. The tensions and ambitions of the American way of life also are blamed. Too often the emphasis is on a better and bigger home and car, more money, more leisure, more television, more spectator sport, more elevators and escalators, less exercise, less action. What we consider to be the best things in life too often are dangerous, as well as fattening and immoral, and we die more quickly than many others.

The kind of work we do has an average mortality rate, too. One study, reported in the *American Journal of Public Health* in 1970, showed that the prominent professionals and businessmen listed in the 1950–1951 edition of *Who's Who in America* lived on the average longer than men in the general population. There are, however, differences within professions. Another study, of all American men who died in 1950 between the ages of twenty and sixty-four, showed that chemists, teachers, engineers, doctors, social workers, agricultural workers, government officials, mail carriers, carpenters, mechanics, tool and die makers, welders, garment workers and household help were among the "healthier" occupations. Those with "average" mortality included medical and dental technicians, accountants, bookkeepers, artists, insurance agents, blacksmiths, compositors and typesetters, railroad engineers, plumbers, reporters and editors, and leather goods workers. A high mortality was found among musicians and music teachers, shoe repairmen, policemen and firemen, waiters, janitors, bartenders, real estate agents, bakers, machinists, tailors, mine workers, metal workers, barbers, fishermen and longshoremen.

Statistical data accumulated from another study, this one a thirteen-year investigation on aging, has also indicated that work satisfaction and a positive attitude toward life may influence our life-spans. In the study of 270 volunteers between sixty and ninety-four years at Duke University, Dr. Erdman Palmore found that those who were satisfied with their work and were optimistic in their attitudes lived longer than those who were pessimistic about their jobs. "We know that mind affects the body in various ways," concluded Dr. Palmore, "We don't completely understand why. But we can see further evidence from this study that a relationship exists between the mental state of the person and his physical condition. It would seem that the best way to increase longevity is to maintain a useful and satisfying role in society, keep a cheerful disposition, remain physically sound and refrain from smoking." One example from the study: an eighty-one-year-old man had an actuarial life expectancy of 5.6 years. His health was average, but his work satisfaction rating was the highest possible. The man was expected to survive 9.5 years on the basis of the study guidelines, but he lived another 11.6 years, more than double the actuarial prediction.

The belief that a person will live longer if he keeps busy when old age comes on has also gained some scientific support. Some years ago, in an experimental program with nursing home patients in Canada, the elderly were divided into two groups. One group received normal nursing home care; the members of the other were urged to dress and feed themselves and to indulge in activities instead of staying in bed and being waited on. Handicrafts and hobbies were made available. A year after the program began, 64 per cent of the active group were still alive, compared to 45 per cent of the inactive group. According to the medical director of the Vancouver General Hospital, Dr. L. E. Ranta, 18 per cent of the active group had improved so much they were discharged. Only 5 per cent of the inactive patients were allowed to leave the home.

Physical activity prior to the time old age arrives may also have something to do with postponing death. A study of former outstanding Finnish long-distance runners and cross-country skiers whose ages ranged from forty to seventy-nine, for instance, showed that they had "younger" cardiopulmonary systems than a comparable group from the members of a shopkeepers' association. A related longevity study of 388 former athletes showed a median life expectancy of seventy-two years, six to seven years longer than that of the general population above age fifteen. Dr. Jean Mayer, professor of nutrition at Harvard University and chairman of a 1969 White House Conference on Food, Nutrition and Health, a few years ago listed six major factors responsible for the "explosive increase in death from heart disease" among men and women in the world's more highly civilized countries. He identified these as lack of exercise, obesity, a high-fat diet among sedentary people, such as office workers, untreated high blood pressure, cigarette smoking and excessive fatigue. Activity and avoidance of overweight were the key points in Dr. Mayer's program to prevent the onset of heart disease such as atherosclerosis. In atherosclerosis, or hardening of the arteries, there is a buildup of fatty material in the smooth inner wall of the coronary arteries, small blood vessels about the size of a straw that carry blood to nourish the heart muscle. When the blood flow to the heart is slowed down or cut off, a heart attack occurs. Studies have indicated that diets high in fats raise the levels of a fatlike substance, cholesterol, in the blood, and the pile-up in the arteries begins. It is believed that regular exercise improves blood circulation in the body, including blood flow to the heart. Blood cholesterol and the blood fat, triglyceride, both tend to be lowered with activity.

Heredity, also, may be responsible for some longer life-spans. For example, if either parent has had heart disease, the offspring's chances of developing it are greater — four times greater, according to one study. It is heredity that affects the size of the blood-carrying arteries, thereby determining whether a person is prone to a heart attack. It is our genes, the basic units of heredity, that are responsible for such disorders as hemophilia and diabetes, and, by actual count, some fifteen hundred other conditions. Scientists also have been able to demonstrate that it is sometimes better to have a long-living father in the family than a long-living mother. One study showed that the offspring of parents where the father was ninety and over and the mother died between sixty and seventy-nine were more likely to be still alive at age seventy than the offspring of ninety-year-old mothers and of fathers who died earlier. (In the Duke study mentioned earlier, however, longevity did not seem to be genetically related since the longevity quotient — the number of years the individual survived after the study divided by the expected number of years according to actuarial tables based on age and sex — showed no correlation with the parents' ages at death.)

Science aside for a moment, the reasons given by people who have lived exceptionally long lives — that is, over one hundred — are of interest. There was, for instance, Shirali Mislimov of Russia, believed to have been the oldest person in the world when he died at one hundred and sixty in 1966. Mislimov worked until his death as a watchman on a farm, riding his donkey over five miles of mountain slopes to work each day. He fathered his last child at the age of one hundred and thirty, and, according to the doctors, had a blood pressure typical of a man in his thirties. He had various explanations for his longevity, depending on who asked him. He told one interviewer that it was "Allah and the Soviet Power," another that it was "lots of children and a good nature," and a third that it was pure air and water, no alcohol and no smoking. There was Professor Frederick Starr, a noted anthropologist, who said on the occasion of his retirement at the age of seventy from the University of Chicago in 1923, "I may say that I not only expect to live to be a hundred and twenty, but that I definitely will live to a hundred and twenty. It is written in my destiny. My mother lived to be ninety-six, her father lived to eighty-three, her grandfather to eighty-seven. I belong to that branch of the family." Dr. Starr said also that he lived a "free life, often staying up till midnight," did not diet and exercised only by walking. (The professor did not live to be a hundred and twenty.)

"Anyone can attain longevity providing they have nothing constitutionally wrong with them and will follow simple rules," remarked Mrs. Deborah Stillman of Connecticut just before she celebrated her hundred and eighth birthday in 1908. "Eat plain food, wear plain clothes, retire early and rise with the sun, avoid the use of stimulants and follow an occupation which keeps the body and mind occupied."

Not everyone believed in a life of abstention. Joshua Seitlein, Brooklyn's oldest inhabitant in 1909 at one hundred and five, drank three pints of whiskey and six glasses of beer a day, and smoked strong Russian pipe tobacco. A man who witnessed Napoleon's retreat from Moscow, Seitlein said he never worried, "because it gives you wrinkles and destroys your appetite," rose early, talked only of cheerful things, laughed as much as he could, and consumed a good deal of strong tea, a mixture of potatoes and fat, and a concoction of herrings and sweet oil. Tilden Pierce, the oldest man in Plymouth County, Massachusetts, back in 1911, had the answer to why we don't live as long as our grandfathers and great-grandfathers. "What's shortening the days of the present generation," he said at his one hundredth birthday party, "is because they eats too much pie and cake. Pie and cake is no more fit to eat than poison, but the boys and girls gobbles them down as much as they can get a hold of. Then, look at the number of times a fellow bathes these days. Why, some of 'em are always at it. But it's a dangerous practice and bound to sap a fellow's strength. If a man allows himself to become so unclean that he has to have a bath twice a week, well, he'd better look out or he'll soon be dead." And there was Mrs. Maschi Urdang, celebrating her birthday in New York in 1922, whose prescription for a long life was a simple one: "I don't have any rules. That's why I'm a hundred and twelve."

Centenarians still are a rarity, but the time may come when man's life-span will reach one hundred years without a prescription. Some say it will happen before this century ends. How will science accomplish this? Will we break the seventy-year barrier by simply replacing worn-out body parts with transplanted, healthier organs and artificial organs? Or can science interfere directly with the aging process that slowly and surely dims our sight, unsteadies our steps, and narrows our mental horizons?

Some scientists argue that merely extending human

life in the same tired old body is not the answer. There is a difference between a longer life, and a longer period of vigor. One can go back to Greek mythology for an analogy in the tale of Eos and Tithonus. Eos, daughter of the Titans Theia and Hyperion, was known as "rosy-fingered Morn," the personification of the dawn of morning. She loved all fresh, young life, and when she was attracted to a handsome youth she carried him off and obtained immortal life for him. Tithonus became her husband, but when she asked Zeus to give him immortality she forgot to add to her request "and eternal youth." Tithonus became old and helpless, and Eos, to avoid the sight of his infirmity, shut him up in a chamber where, it was said, he turned into a chirping grasshopper. The story demonstrates that it might be wrong to lengthen life with, say, the use of spare parts, if the rest of the body is worn away and of no use to the owner. Few would want to live in such a body.

Then, too, scientists point out, even if science found cures for the leading causes of death — heart disease, cancer and stroke — and wars and accidents were somehow eliminated, the average life expectancy might only rise to about eighty, not much of a gain. "If every other medical problem now under attack were solved," concluded the noted chemist Dr. Johan Bjorksten a few years ago, "the average life expectancy would still not be increased more than approximately fifteen years. For example, a person who would be saved from dying of cancer or coronary disease at the age of ninety would have been so weakened at age one hundred and five that any trivial cause would terminate his life. Thus, the most that could be gained if all other medical projects were 100 per cent successful would be about fifteen years of increasingly precarious existence."

Since there does appear to be a definite limit on how long we live, and since all of us are dying a little bit every day of our lives, many scientists are moving away from trying to turn man into a mere robot, kept alive and moving by plastic hearts and electronic brains. We have seen that our life-style — environmental and psychological — can work to slow down, to some extent, the aging process, and help to keep us healthier and alive longer. If such factors do the trick, some scientists believe, might not a biological and chemical approach also slow up the clock, change minutes into hours, give us a longer period of active life?

Aging, according to scientists, seems to be a cumulative result of wear and tear on the human machine. But where, exactly, in just what part of the body, does it begin? Speculation has it that aging occurs at the level of the smallest unit of life, the cell. In some people, the cells lose their talent for regenerating; they die more quickly, and are replaced too slowly — or never. With muscle and nerve cells gone, the equipment which runs our bodies then becomes worn out and creaky. With no new parts to lend a hand, the body becomes less capable of fighting off infections and repairing accident and stress damages. Life ends when our cells run out of energy. The big question is why the cells fail in the first place. There are many theories. One is that cellular life-span is a function of the environment in which the cell lives, and that a cell is potentially immortal if a satisfactory environment is maintained for it. There is the theory that the mysterious mechanism that causes aging is hidden away in the genes. This has led to speculation that there is a structural change in the genes with aging, and that the aging process might be controlled by transplanting DNA (the stuff of life in the cell) from a young person to an older person. Genes undergoing structural changes causing aging could be stopped immediately.

Dr. Bjorksten is the author of an exciting theory known as cross-linkage. This deals with basic activities of body chemistry at the molecular level, where a myriad of chemical parts intermesh and become a working whole. The theory holds that more and more molecules — the smallest physical units of an element or compound — become cross-linked as life goes on. The accumulation slows down or stops the activity of essential molecules and interferes with normal biochemical activity. Dr. Bjorksten has said that the only way in which dramatic control of aging can be achieved is to find means to break down the cross-linked molecules in the cells.

Other gerontologists — scientists in pursuit of the elusive secret of aging — have turned to collagen chemistry. Collagen is the protein that makes up about 40 per cent of all the protein in the body, and many researchers feel that the aging of this collagen is not unrelated to the stiffness of joints and the leatheriness of skin which afflicts the elderly. The substance of tendon and cartilage, collagen fills the space between muscle fibers and between the cells, thus serving as the stabilizing fiber of connective tissue. A thick matting of collagen in the skin gives the skin its characteristic toughness and plasticity. This is the material which becomes the substance of leather after tanning. The investigations of leather chemists, therefore, have made significant contributions to gerontology, and it is felt that collagen chemistry may open the door to discovery of substances that promote the cross-linking and thus, the aging of collagen in the body. Research also has focused on a pigment known as lipofuscin that seems to settle in aging tissues. By thickening there, scientists believe, it may stop the cells from performing their normal chores. In broad terms, then, that phenomenon we know as aging probably resides in cells or molecules, or in both.

One of the world's foremost researchers in gerontology is Dr. Alex Comfort, head of the Medical Research Council Group on Aging at University College, London, who has launched experiments to determine whether life may be prolonged by administering certain drugs. It is easier, Dr. Comfort believes, to postpone disease than it is to prevent or cure it. Dr. Comfort has suggested that there may be a biological clock that could be tampered with, and slowed down, thereby postponing most of all the deteriorative changes that affect individuals. The aging process, he suggests, may be like a phonograph record that, once played, cannot be replayed; the performance can only be prolonged by running the record more slowly, but not so much slower that the music is spoiled. Or if the aging process is one of "noise accumulation" — like the noise that accumulates in a record with years of playing — maybe all that is necessary is that the needle be kept clean, Dr. Comfort believes.

At a recent International Congress of Gerontology, it was suggested that substances which chemists add to cereal and rubber tires to prevent them from spoiling may be the key to prolongation of human life. Experiments with the chemicals already have resulted in a 40 per cent increase in the life-spans of mice. The substances are what scientists call antioxidants — chemical "scavengers" that mop up the agents that spoil lard and other foods and cause automobile tires to deteriorate. One of the substances, known as BHT, is added to breakfast cereals in small amounts. Vitamin E, a natural antioxidant, also has been found to have a like effect. In other experiments, researchers found that cutting back on calories could double the life-span of laboratory rats. "We feel certain," says Dr. Comfort, "that diet from childhood on plays a very important role in the aging process." Scientists also have studied microscopic animals known as rotifers which live in fresh and salt water and go through a whole life cycle in twenty days. By changing the water temperature and the animal's nutrition, researchers have been able to regulate its aging rate. Scientists working at the Oak Ridge National Laboratory have taken a different route. They took spleen cells from mice — the spleen is an abdominal organ which manufactures, stores and destroys blood cells —

and injected them into other mice, whose life-spans, they found, can thereby be extended by a third. Other research at the laboratory has suggested that disease-fighting cells might be removed from a young person, deep-frozen, and then injected later in life, allowing the body's capacity to battle infection to be raised. Theoretically, this would work because doctors know that most people die of infection rather than "old age."

Several investigators, taking a cue from the process of hibernation in which certain animals pass the cold months in a sleeplike state, have been able to retard aging and boost the life-spans of several kinds of animals by dropping the normal body temperature. During natural hibernation, animals such as woodchucks, ground squirrels and dormice have their body temperatures reduced to near the freezing point, and have very slow heartbeats and respirations. It is known that bats that hibernate regularly seem to live much longer than those that hibernate occasionally. The desert mouse, which goes into a state similar to hibernation but during hot, dry months, may live up to four times longer than the laboratory mouse. Scientists speculate that if drugs could be developed which would set the body's thermostat at a lower temperature, the human life span might be lengthened by twenty or so years.

But the ultimate in the use of lowered temperatures is a controversial technique, not yet proven, called cryonics. This is a method by which a person who has died is deep-frozen until the time comes when medical science finds a cure for the disease that killed him. When that happens, according to cryonics enthusiasts, the body will be thawed out, treated for the disease, and brought back to life. Many scientists doubt cryonics ever will work because deep-freezing has a violent effect on cellular structure. The delicate chemical and physical makeup of the cells would be so damaged that it would be exceedingly difficult, if not impossible, to restore life. Thus far, no one has been able to revive a single frozen organ, let alone anything so complex as a man.

And so the quest continues. Immortality still is not within our grasp, nor is anyone sure it ever will be. There might well be an inherent limit to life, a road block that man has nearly reached. And if there is such a barrier, man, with all his sciences, will never drive through it.

It could be, when all is finished here, when all is said and done, when there are no more rivers to ford and no more mountains to scale, that immortality will be found, not on earth, not here and now, but in another place, in another time, in a form we find it difficult to imagine. But if man ever does succeed in breaking the life-barrier here on earth, if he does succeed in his search for the unlimited horizon, he will need to have done more than remember to ask for what Eos forgot, more than simply to rejoice at the achievement. The gift of longer life carries with it the responsibility to see to it that the extra years which have been sought and won will be paid for with a better world in which to live those years.

Ten

The Hereafter

What happens when we die? Is death the end of everything, a state of nonexistence whose only pain is that felt by the grieving survivors? Or is it the escape from our earthly bodies of a soul that lives on somehow, somewhere, in something? Are we reincarnated as men or women, boys or girls, animals or trees? Are our souls resurrected from the grave on a day of judgment, or doomed to roam the earth, like the Flying Dutchman, on an endless trip? And what of the nature of the soul itself, that elusive spirit, as difficult to catch as a wreath of smoke, as hard to find as the back of the mind. Does it exist? In short, is death an ending — or a beginning?

Eschatology, the branch of theology that deals with these matters, and a belief that there is a life after death are part of the religion and culture of many peoples. Unfortunately, since no one has been to the otherworld and returned to discuss his impressions, man's ideas of what happens after death have been shaped by his religious and personal beliefs, by his needs and by the other influences that mold his mind and life. Science has been of little or no help in answering his questions, one way or the other. And religion, for all its pronouncements that there is certainly some sort of life afterward, must rely heavily on various concepts of God, on Scripture and other sacred writings and, in the final analysis, on faith, a gift from God that one can accept or reject.

The Hereafter

The soul, or spirit, has fascinated man almost as long as he has walked on earth. Cave paintings and sculptured figurines of the Stone Age, thousands of years before the birth of Christ, attest to a simple concept of life after death. There is archaeological evidence that Cro-Magnon man, the prototype of modern European man who lived between 60,000 and 10,000 B.C., believed the cave paintings of the animals he had killed in the hunt held their souls. These early men placed gifts before the crude drawings to apologize for having hunted them, and they performed ritual dances in front of them in the hope of gaining the strength of the dead animals.

Many have spoken authoritatively about the existence of the soul and a life in the hereafter. Ironically, a goodly number of the statements have been made by people with little or no knowledge of the very world they live in. In the beginning, the soul was supposed to be a material thing, identified with the breath or the blood, or located in the bowels, the bones, the liver. Heraclitus taught that it was a "fiery vapor," Seneca that it was a god dwelling in the human form, and the Basutos of Africa were careful not to let their shadows fall on the water for fear of drowning. The verses of the English poet Sir John Davies call to mind many of the early Greek opinions about the soul:

> One thinks the soule is aire; another fire;
> Another blood, diffus'd about the heart;
> Another saith the elements conspire,
> And to her essence each doth give a part.

Musicians thinke our soules are harmonies;
Physicians hold that they complexions be;
Epicures make them swarmes of atomies,
Which doth by chance into our bodies flee.

Later, the notion that the soul was somehow linked to the brain, to our personalities and to our general thought processes came into vogue. Many began to feel that "the name of soule is vaine, and that we onely well-mixt bodies are." Aristotle made the soul little more than a faculty or attribute of the body, comparing it to "the axness of an ax." Aquinas accepted the Aristotelian view, defining man and personality as a composite of body and soul, matter and form. The French philosopher René Descartes believed the soul was in the pea-sized pineal gland in the lower part of the brain, while other physiologists of the seventeenth century placed it in different organs connected to the brain. "Although the human soul is united to the whole body," Descartes wrote in 1644, "it has, nevertheless, its principal seat in the brain, where alone it not only understands and imagines, but also perceives." Baron Gottfried Leibnitz, a German philosopher and mathematician, theorized that the soul resided at a precise mathematical point.

Nowadays, when we speak of the soul, we generally mean that spiritual part of man distinct from the physical that lives, feels, thinks and wills. Some call it the "ego," or the "self." Others prefer the more poetic phrases, such as "the vital spark," or "the breath of life." Soul has also come to mean the embodiment of some quality — high-mindedness, nobility and courage. We speak of a person as being "the very soul of kindness," or as "a timid soul." Or, we might say that someone "has soul," meaning that he possesses a certain warmth of feeling. Some also regard the soul as God Himself, or the attributes of God in man.

Animals and even plants have been thought to have souls. The term animism (derived from the Latin *anima*, meaning breath or soul) refers to the doctrine of the reality of souls. True animists believe that natural objects, natural phenomena and even the universe have souls. Thus, we find a number of places mentioned by both primitive and more sophisticated cultures as the dwelling places of souls: sticks and stones, sun and moon, birds and bees, fire and wind, rivers, lakes and mountain streams. Many animists differentiated between souls and spirits, believing that souls were souls only as long as they remained in the bodies of live humans and animals. At death, they left these bodies, changed into spirits or ghosts, and sought out new abodes — either other bodies, or natural objects. Natives of the Malay Peninsula, for example, believed that roof beams and kitchen utensils were possessed by spirits; consequently, when a homeowner died and a new owner moved in, there were long and involved rituals which included burying the household vessels with the deceased so that the spirits could accompany him.

The Aztecs believed that the souls of their warriors slain in battle, as well as those of women who died in childbirth, went to the sun. Savages of Borneo thought there were seven souls in every man and that they flew from the body at death through the big toe — in the shape of a butterfly. Other peoples believed the souls of friends and relatives lingered near the scene of their former lives, depending on the living for food and remembrance. In a Greek burial custom, wine was poured on the grave to quench the thirst of the dead, and animals were sacrificed for the soul's food. Only the kindest terms were used to describe the deceased during the banquet in his honor because, it was believed, the soul was present at the feast. The ancient Chinese honored their ancestors by making statues of them and consulting these for guidance, a practice that is at the basis of modern Asian ancestor-worship. Today, all over southeast Asia, one can find elaborately carved and decorated "spirit houses," where spirits of the dead can live and be appeased. Among the Greenland Eskimos, there is the belief that man is made up of a body, a soul and his name. When man dies, his soul, about the size of a finger, finds new life as an animal, in the sea or sky. The name returns from the grave when it is given to a newborn babe.

Animal worship grew out of animism, and became part of the practice of a number of religions. The Egyptians, for example, worshiped the bull and a cat-headed goddess. The Greeks had Pan, a goat-god, and the American Indians revered the bear. In Thailand, the elephant is still a holy object.

That animism and religion are closely intertwined is fairly obvious, but there is a difference of opinion over whether religion grew out of the widespread notion that souls were everywhere, in everything. Sir Edward B. Tylor, the noted British anthropologist, was one who tried to prove that religion did, in fact, actually spring from animism, that man established religion in order to have a link between himself and the spirits he believed were all around him. Primitive men, according to Tylor, wondered about the difference between a living body and a dead one. They asked themselves what caused waking, sleeping, trances, disease and death. They wanted to know about the shapes that peopled their dreams. Tylor concluded: "Looking at these groups of phenomena, the ancient savage philosophers probably made their first step by the obvious inference that every man has two things belonging to him: namely a life, and a phantom." It was this phantom, or soul, that entered into other bodies and objects, and it was man's realization of this that created religion. Religion, according to Tylor, could be defined as a belief in spiritual beings.

Impressive though it was, Tylor's theory was roundly criticized. The whole idea of "ancient savage philosophers" inventing religion because they wanted to answer questions about death and dreams and because they believed everything was alive was seen as too simple. Religion and a belief in the hereafter, after all, went deeper than that. These things had more to do with man's emotions and with his behavior in times of stress. They were personal things, difficult to reconcile with the spirits that Tylor said "possessed, pervaded and crowded" the universe of ancient man. Then, too, Tylor's definition of religion would exclude those philosophical-religious systems that were based not so much on a belief in spiritual beings but on a way of life, a set of values, or man's relationship to the universe and nature. In Confucianism, one of the great religions of China, for instance, more stress was laid on how men should act toward one another than on God. Confucius was never worshiped or honored as a personal god, nor did he ever claim divinity, and his followers preached and practiced his golden rule: "Do not do to others what you do not want done to yourself." And there were the primitive tribes who believed in spirits but did not make them a part of their religious life and ceremonies; they were simply another kind of person, like the forest demons of the Ona Indians of Tierra del Fuego which preyed on the natives but which could be driven off by arrows.

Tylor's critics also felt that because man attributed an "aliveness" to various objects didn't mean he believed these inanimate things had souls of their own. Rather, many primitives believed in a vague, powerful and impersonal force that charged persons and objects, much as an electric current charges the appliances and equipment of our daily lives. The natives of the South Seas called this force mana. Its presence was responsible for everything from good crops to intelligence; its absence, for evil, failure, dull-wittedness. Mana was a kind of communicable energy, not a soul, that could be conveyed from one to another. For instance, a warrior could build up his own supply of mana by killing many enemies; or he could be successful in battle by carrying an amulet that contained the mana of a deceased hero.

Generally, primitive man probably had no deep concept of a soul that lived a separate, material existence — feeling, thinking and willing. For him, there was no clear line between the spirit world and the natural world. Everything was alive, particularly those things that behaved in a curious way. Nothing was really material or static. Seasons came and went, and came back again. The earth quaked and split apart, mountains exploded and spewed fire and molten rock, the winds blew, rain fell, all sorts of things grew. Babies and animals and insects were born, they weakened, and they died. Mana, or call it what you will, was everywhere, charging the universe, making it behave in various ways, and man did not probe it too deeply, if at all. His religion, if it might be called that, was part of his daily life, so closely intertwined with it that there was no way of separating it out — there were religious rites and rituals for virtually everything, from hunting to marriage — and instead of a rationalized doctrine based on abstracts he made use of myths and folklore to explain and perpetuate his beliefs, because it was what he saw that he could believe in. Some of his gods, for example, such as those of ancient Greece, were conceived in the shape of magnified, non-natural men, not as shapeless entities living in some shadowy world.

Religions, as we know them, probably sprang up later in cultures which saw a marked difference between the mind and the environment, between the spirit and nature. Man began to think about the order in nature and in the universe, and the more he thought about it the more he came to believe that there was too much of it to be a chance happening, that it must have been instigated and maintained by someone of higher intelligence. This someone was God, all-wise, all-powerful, a righteous judge separate from the natural world He created. Conceptions of this supreme or absolute being vary widely. There is theism, most fully developed in Christianity, which regards God as a personal, moral being, author and ruler of the universe. Theists do not reject supernatural revelation in arriving at their belief in God. Deism, on the other hand, is a belief in the existence of God, but it is based solely on the evidence of reason and nature and it rejects revelation. Pantheism denies God's personality, and closely identifies Him with nature and the universe. Atheism, of course, denies the existence of God.

A number of arguments have been put forth for the existence of God. Among these is the so-called ontological argument of St. Anselm of Canterbury (1033–1109), an Italian-born philosopher. Anselm taught that since existence was a perfection, and since there were gradations of perfection, God must exist because He represented the absolute perfection. (Since there were gradations of perfection in the world, these meant that there had to be an absolute perfection, God.) The cosmological argument of Aristotle and Aquinas held that because there was a cause for every effect in the world, this chain must eventually reach back to a Prime Cause,

God, because an endless string of causes is not conceivable. The teleological argument arose from the arrangement of the universe and the idea that without an orderer there could be no order. The German philosopher Immanuel Kant (1724–1804) stated a moral argument, holding that because moral law was inherent in human nature there had to be a lawgiver. Some modern-day thinkers, influenced by the scientific theory that the universe was born in one violent upheaval — the so-called Big Bang Theory — argue that some extracosmic force, God, had a hand in it.

Generally, it is the goal of religions, whether they accept one God, or many or none, to attain the highest possible good for mankind. In one sense, religion is a way of life based on man's relationship to God or the universe. In another, it is belief in a divinely created universe to which man must adjust his life in order to achieve eternal salvation, or liberation.

There are many concepts of what form salvation takes. And there are many ways to get there. It might be an impersonal kind of salvation, such as that of the early Greeks and Jews, who believed in a collective form of immortality, of this world, surviving in the memory of the people. It might be the immortality of an individual soul, but a soul without consciousness or feeling, a soul that either is united with the God-force or simply exists by itself, unfeeling, unaware of itself. Or it might be the more personal kind of immortality, with the soul conscious of a heaven or hell, in which it dwells; this belief arose as man became more and more aware of himself as

an individual and not so much a member of a tribe or
herd, as he began to feel that he, as a person, would be
saved or doomed, that there had to be some part of him
that continued on after death. It seemed inconceivable
that something as complex and alive as a human being
could be extinguished forever; if this were so, there
would be no point in life, and there was too much of a
pattern, too much order, too much structure for this to
be so.

The belief that a soul moves on to other bodies,
known as transmigration, forms the basis of many religions. There are the simple forms of primitive animists,
but there are also more involved ideas. In a famous dia-
logue, *Phaedo*, written about the fourth century B.C.,
Plato discussed the immortality of the soul and its ability to be reborn again and again. He argued that everything in nature followed cycles and patterns: heat
became cold, cold became heat, people went to sleep,
they woke up. It was then right to assume that this same
kind of cycling applied to dying and returning to life;
just as the living died, so, too, did the dead come back to
life. If this were not the case, said Plato, life would soon
disappear from the universe. He also argued that all
learning and experience were really recollections of
ideas we knew before, in another life; man was constantly being reminded of something. Ideas, for Plato,
were immaterial patterns fixed in nature, different from
the phenomena around us. True reality was not in the
particular animal, tree or person that we saw, but in the
idea of those things. Individual objects in any one nat-

ural class were imperfect copies of the ideas, and only fleeting and perishable substances that drew their being from the ideas. In his daily life, man was constantly aware of certain ideals — scientific and moral — for which there was no seeming explanation. Therefore, said Plato, we must have known them before we inhabited our present bodies, before our birth.

One religion that believes in transmigration is Hinduism, the traditional faith of India with some four million followers. In Hinduism there is an absolute power called Brahma. It is the goal of all mankind to be united with this force, for it is only then that man will be perfect. But first, the soul must be reborn over and over again until it is pure enough to join with Brahma. The return of the soul to Brahma comes from the idea of *karma*, a belief that a person's destiny is decided by what he does in life. If he lives like an animal and is guilty of misdeeds, he will return to earth in an animal's body. If his life has been decent he will be reborn, reincarnated, as a human being; but he can be rich or poor, a prince or a farmer, beautiful or ugly. Whatever his character was in the last life, that is what it will be in the next.

Another religion like Hinduism is Buddhism, founded in India by Gautama Buddha (560–480 B.C.). With a hundred and ninety million adherents, mostly in China, Japan and southeast Asia, Buddhism teaches that life's pain and suffering are caused by desire, and that the only way to end the misery is through enlightenment. (Buddha means Fully Enlightened One, or Awakened One). Buddhists pursue an Eightfold Path of righteous living — right understanding, right motives, right speech, right action, right vocation, right effort, right mindfulness and right contemplation — before they are purified enough to achieve the state known as Nirvana. This term has been variously understood. Some have regarded it as a final extinction of human individuality and personality, like the blowing out of a flame. Others see it as the extinction of individual passion and hatred, or as a state of holiness, perfect peace, and wisdom, with freedom from the long chain of rebirths. Like Hindus, Buddhists believe that the human soul descends into animals, plants and other forms of life. Buddha himself, before his final rebirth as Sakyamuni, went through as many as five hundred and fifty births — he was, among other things, a hermit, king, ape, slave, elephant, snipe, fish, frog and tree. When he reached the state of perfect knowledge, he was able to recall all these lives, some of which are described in a collection of fables called the Jatakas.

Two other offshoots of Hinduism, Jainism and Sikhism, also believe that the soul is reborn into many bodies before it becomes good enough to be joined to the infinite. Jainism, founded in India, is a good deal like Buddhism. It teaches that even the lowly insect is sacred, and forbids its followers to do harm to any living creature. Atheists, Jains deny the possibility of a perfect being existing through all eternity. Animate beings, however, are composed of soul and body and the souls are eternal — a point of departure from Buddhism. After a soul has inhabited many bodies, Jains believe, it frees itself and lives happily. Nirvana, to them, is endless blessedness. Sikhism, a blend of Hinduism and Islam, the faith of Moslems, was begun in India as a politico-religious system, and was based on the principle of monotheism and human brotherhood. Religious fanatics, Sikhs were forbidden to return the salutations of Hindus and were bound to kill Moslems on meeting them. The Holy War was their vocation, and Sikh soldiers prayed to their swords. Transmigration was central to Sikhism.

Another route to salvation, one that does not revolve around the belief in transmigration, is that central to religions such as Christianity, Islam and Zoroastrianism. These three faiths, founded many centuries apart, preach that man's deeds on earth will be judged by a supreme deity, and that man's soul will be sent either to a place of reward, a heaven, or damned to eternal punishment in a hell.

Zoroastrianism, founded in 600 B.C. by the Persian religious teacher Zoroaster, probably had a good deal of influence on Christianity and Judaism, but this is disputed by some scholars. The religion focused on Ahura-Mazda, god of light, and taught that good thoughts, good deeds and good words were the object of moral striving. Man receives his eternal reward in heaven by fighting on the side of Ahura-Mazda in the cosmic struggle between good and evil for mastery of the universe, which will end in the defeat of the powers of darkness. Those who choose the wrong side will be damned in the final judgment of the dead. Interestingly, the religion teaches that Zoroaster received a code of laws from Ahura-Mazda on Mount Sabalan, much as Moses received the Ten Commandments from Jehovah on Mount Sinai. Ahura-Mazda himself, of course, parallels Jehovah, and Ahriman, the prince of darkness, is similar to Satan. The Zoroastrian first period of creation is divided into six parts, as the story of the Creation in the Old Testament is divided into six days. The religion also had its Adam and Eve in Moshya and Moshyana, and a catastrophe similar to the deluge sent by God to punish mankind — Ahura-Mazda created a terrible winter. Zoroastrians also celebrate high and low masses and include water, milk and bread in their ceremonies, much as some Christians use wine, water and bread in their services.

Islam, founded by the prophet Mohammed (A.D. 570–632), has some four hundred and sixty million adherents, most of them in Africa, the Middle East and Indonesia. Moslems (or Muslims) believe there is one God, Allah, and that Mohammed was his prophet. Islam means peace and submission to God's will. Islam's teachings are found in the Koran, the sacred book which is largely drawn from Jewish and Christian sources (Moses and Jesus are listed among the prophets). There are angels led by the archangel Gabriel, and a day of judgment after which the wicked are sent to hell and the just to a heaven that is full of sensual delights. Christians generally believe that souls are judged after the death of the body and sent to heaven or hell where they will remain until a general resurrection, at which time the souls of the just are reunited to their perfected bodies. Catholics add the doctrine of purgatory to their religion, seeing it as a sort of way station between hell and heaven, where souls with lesser sins are purified before going on to heaven.

Various pictures of heaven and hell have been painted for us down through the ages. Prophets and poets, theologians and philosophers all have tried their hand at locating and describing these spiritual abodes. Heaven for the Greeks was a place of bliss called the Elysian Fields. Homer placed it on the western border of the earth, while other poets located it in the underworld, in a place called Hades where the spirits of all the dead went. Hades was surrounded by fiery rivers, its solitary approach guarded by a monstrous three-headed dog, Cerberus, who prevented spirits from escaping to the upper world. The wicked were sent to Tartarus, a deep and sunless abyss far below Hades. The Hebrews believed in three heavens: the air, the starry firmament and the abode of God. (Traditional Judaism accepts that a Messiah will come to redeem the Jewish people, and there will be a resurrection of the body during the Messiah's advent. This reunion of body and spirit, however, will last only for the Messianic Age, after which the soul will return to heaven.) For the cabalists, mystics who interpreted scripture around the twelfth century, there were seven heavens, each rising in happiness above the preceding one, and to be in Seventh Heaven was to be supremely happy. The Germans had their Valhalla, a warrior's paradise with a golden roof; the

American Indians, their Happy Hunting Ground. In the Old Testament we read of Sheol, a place where good and bad alike were sent after death to live a dim, shadowy, rather inactive existence; souls in Sheol had no consciousness, no individuality, a far cry from the humanized souls that are tortured and feel pain in the inferno of the poet Dante. Gehenna, in the Apocrypha of the New Testament, comes close to the modern theological idea of hell as a place of suffering, although references to it are rather vague.

Today, while some still hold to the classic picture of hell as a place of fire and brimstone where the damned experience physical suffering, a good many Christian theologians see it as a state of being rather than a place, a condition of spiritual distress that is the natural consequence of sin and which is all in the mind. For some, hell is like purgatory, with everyone eventually saved. For still others, the doctrine of conditional immortality teaches that sinners will be completely destroyed while the just survive with God or in some state of eternal blessedness; hell is simply death and the extinction of personality. In Indian religions, hell represents but one phase in the soul's activities and is never regarded as eternal.

Contemporary conceptions of the soul and life after death do not, in the final analysis, differ much from older beliefs. When one comes down to it, most of it has been said before, and our ideas about what happens at the end of mortal life are not really new. It is extremely difficult, probably impossible, to put the soul under a microscope — although many have tried. Science can tell that life is continuous, moving through cells from person to person, and that a new individual emerges out of that endless chain at a certain period. It can also tell us when our hearts and brains die, and there are instruments to prove the fact. But there are no instruments, no experimental data, no computerized equipment to confirm the existence of the soul, a state of heaven and hell, or such a thing as reincarnation. This lies within the realm of philosophical, theological, ethical, and personal belief. Yet, man still tries to find tangible proof, if only, in the words of Sigmund Freud, because in the unconscious "every one of us is convinced of his own immortality." Dr. Joseph B. Rhine, a renowned psychologist who pioneered in studying the mysterious powers of the mind, once said that investigations already had given scientific proof of the existence of a spiritual order of some sort, and that the evidence strongly favored the possibility that there was something about human personality that could survive. Unfortunately, Dr. Rhine wasn't able to discuss, in precise terms, what that evidence was.

In the early twentieth century a number of experiments aimed at proving the soul's existence were performed. Doctors and scientists claimed to have weighed, X-rayed and photographed the soul. Among these were five Massachusetts physicians, "of the highest professional standing" according to the newspaper accounts. After working with patients in a sanatorium for some six years, they reported that when the soul flitted from the

body it diminished the weight of the body by a measurable amount. They found this out, they said, by placing dying patients on a specially constructed platform
balance sensitive to a weight of less than one-tenth of an
ounce. With the patient on one platform of the scale and
a counterweight on the opposite platform, the doctors
waited for death to come. At that moment, they reported, as soon as the heart stopped beating, the platform opposite the one holding the patient "fell with
startling suddenness, just as if something had been lifted
quickly from the body." The simple use of silver dollars
to balance the scale after the patient died, established
that the human soul was a material thing that weighed
from a half-ounce to an ounce. The doctors' discovery
was received with a good bit of skepticism, not to men-
tion outright ridicule. One newspaper wondered why
the doctors weren't able to see the fleeing soul which, if
it weighed as much as an ounce, must have been large
enough to be visible to the naked eye. "It would have
been better if one of them had watched for the soul
itself and let the other four keep their eyes on the scale,"
the paper said with tongue in cheek. "Perhaps the 'five
illustrious physicians' can explain this apparent anom-
aly. If they can, they are more illustrious than we think
they are." William James of Harvard, the noted philosopher and psychologist, commented that the exact moment of death was so very vague as to be difficult to
determine, adding that he would class the theory of the
Massachusetts physicians with "those fantastic cranky
ideas men get hold of sometimes." James's colleague

The Hereafter

Professor Hugo Münsterburg asked that reporters who had called him excuse him from saying even a single word on the subject.

Around the same time, a gentleman named Fournier d'Albe, secretary of the Dublin Society for Psychical Research, theorized that the soul of man is an aggregation of soul particles he called "psychomeres." These could be found in the cells of the body, were probably opaque to ultraviolet light and, theoretically, would one day be made visible by more powerful optical means. D'Albe also speculated that they would be weighed and measured and that their weight probably would be found to be about one-thousandth part of the weight of the body. Put another way, if a person weighed one hundred and fifty pounds, he probably had about two and a half ounces of soul. D'Albe carried his theory even further. After death, he argued, the psychomeres united to form a "soul-body" which escaped into the atmosphere where it floated about. The soul-body had consciousness and lived cheaply, subsisting on the sun's rays. It was not lonely, d'Albe said, because it lived in the "soul realm" (vaguely located between the earth and two hundred miles above it) with the souls of all those who had lived in the past thirty thousand years. But that was not all. Each "soul-body" had a different life-span. When its time was up it underwent another transformation, this time into a state of existence in interplanetary space. There it joined in the final cosmic union of all souls of all ages.

A number of experiments also were undertaken to

remedy the fact that the soul had never been seen. Most researchers operated on the assumption that all human beings possessed "auras." These were composed of some sort of influence, force or filmy matter and were supposed to surround each body as an atmosphere. Clairvoyants, mystics and mediums alleged that these psychic emanations contained the subtle essence of each individual. If these auras could be photographed, this would obviously show them to be physical realities and this is what several scientists tried to do. In 1904, Professor Elmer Gates, director of a laboratory for psychology and "psychurgy" in Maryland, reported on his work with the aura of animals. He used ultraviolet radiation along with a wall coated with a photosensitive substance, rhodopsin, taken from the retina of the eye of a freshly killed animal. Professor Gates found that when he placed inorganic and inanimate substances between the tube emitting the rays and the chemically coated wall no shadow was cast on the sensitized wall. Living creatures, however, were opaque to the rays, and they cast shadows, according to Gates, as long as they retained life. Gates reported that he placed a live rat in a sealed glass tube held in the path of the rays and in front of the chemically treated wall. As long as the rat remained alive, Gates said, it cast a shadow. Killing the animal, however, made it suddenly become "transparent." At the same time, a shadow having precisely the same shape of the animal was seen to pass out through the glass tube and move upward on the sensitized wall. As it approached the top of the wall, the shadow grew dimmer, until it disappeared. Gates concluded: "Now if in any way this escaping organism could be caught and made to give evidence that it still possessed mind, then we would for the first time have an inductive laboratory proof of the continuity of life after death." (A few years earlier, Gates made the astonishing announcements that he could photograph thoughts in the human mind, had discovered a way of cleansing the mind of a criminal with the light rays, and had demonstrated that microbes could think.)

Three years after Gates's experiments were made public, Dr. Hippolyte Baraduc, a French physician, published photographs purporting to be "human emanations," taken while the subjects were praying. The photos, which resemble swirling fog and filmy cloud patches, were said to represent prayer winging its way heavenward, a curative force at Lourdes during a miracle, a benediction flowing from the upraised hands of a priest at an altar, and a soul in religious fervor. Later, Dr. Baraduc claimed to have photographed the departing soul of his wife at the time of her death. He described this as a "nebulous globe" and explained he was able to take the picture because the aura surrounding human beings survives as long as eighty hours after death. "Man," said Dr. Baraduc, "does not belong to this planet only, but to the starry spaces in which his thoughts revolve."

Dr. Patrick S. O'Donnell, a Chicago X-ray expert, continued the aura experiments, and claimed to have witnessed "the flight of the vital spark" from a dying patient. He accomplished this, he declared, by peering at his subject through a chemically coated glass screen. In his own words: "Last night, I tried the experiment on a dying man. He was rapidly sinking. Suddenly the attending physician announced that the man was dead. The aura began to spread from the body and presently disappeared. Further observations of the corpse revealed no sign of the aura. We do not claim that the light is the soul or the spirit. In fact, no one seems to know what it is. In my opinion, however, it is some sort of radioactivity made visible by the use of the chemical screen. My experiments, however, seem to prove that it is the animating power or current of life of human beings." Earlier, a Dr. Walter J. Kilner of London, who had invented a screen for viewing the human halo, reported that it could be used to diagnose illness. When disease is present, he said, the auras were irregular and broken; the aura of an epileptic was misshapen, especially about the head; and that of the dyspeptic showed as "shaky lines" around the stomach. In men, Dr. Kilner declared, the auras were considerably alike; but in women, they had different shapes, particularly in the transition period between childhood and womanhood.

Others of the period, not of a scientific bent, claimed also to have seen the soul as it fled the body. Among these was a New Jersey woman, Mrs. David Baldwin, who insisted that she saw the soul of her father-in-law escape from his body in the form of a butterfly. As she told it: "I stood there spellbound as there issued from his lips the apparition of mystic gray light that formed itself clearly into spreading wings, each, I should say, about a foot long. The thing was so tangible, so real that my first thought was to seize it. I can only explain it as being supernatural." At about the same time, one Henry Price of New York made the newspapers by asserting: "The soul of a man is soft and gelatinous, small, practically shapeless, and situated beneath the first rib. Below the Adam's apple in a man, and in a woman at the base of her throat is a spot of little or no resistance. It is from this place, when the hour of death has come, that the soul must be taken."

Some even claimed to have experienced their own soul's flight. Mrs. Baker P. Lee, a Los Angeles clergyman's wife, firmly believed her disembodied spirit traveled into the hereafter and returned. As Mrs. Lee told her experience in 1914: "I saw my husband come in and I tried to open my eyes but could not. I said to myself, 'I am not dead,' but I was powerless to move. Then my four children were brought in weeping. Then my father stepped into the room, just as he used to in life. He and I were chums. I said, 'I'm not dead.' He replied, 'Not yet, not yet.' Suddenly I felt my spirit leaving my body. It was gone in an instant, leaping out, a joyous, light and exhilarating release of the very essence of life into space. My form remained the same, but the substance had utterly changed. It was now a translucent vapor, capable, at my will, of going immediately to any place. I possessed all my faculties, imagination, will and memory. I was among the clouds, knowing the joy of flight. Then I came down and hovered over the city, saw the people and wished to be able to reveal myself to some to let them know that life after death is beautiful."

These attempts to explain the soul in physical terms soon went out of style. The belief that the soul left the body in some visible guise was, after all, an ancient one, probably some four thousand years old. There had been everything from angels speeding through space on wings, to the Greeks' personification of the soul, Psyche, who flew about on gauzy butterfly wings, to the soul pictured in the Egyptian Book of the Dead as a man with outspread wings hovering at the head of a mummy on its funeral bed.

Reincarnation is an old idea, too, but it keeps reappearing down through the years, and not only among Buddhists and Hindus. Even today, informed laymen of many faiths or of no faith, along with reputable scientists and an assortment of eccentrics and fakers are strongly impressed by the theory that people living now lived at another time. Reincarnation does have a certain logical quality that appeals to many, a quality that is missing in visions of winged spirits, souls made of jelly and harp-playing angels. It is argued that heredity and environment often do not explain why people act the way they do, and that many people seem to have recollections of things they could not have known if they had not experienced them.

Reincarnation also is used often to explain the biological conception of atavism, which is the reappearance in an individual of characteristics of some remote ancestor that have been absent for generations. Biologists say it is the result of a recombination of genes which did not occur in the immediate ancestors. The English naturalist Charles Darwin noticed that it often followed the crossing of a species. Certain kinds of tame rabbits, for example, can be crossed to produce the reappearance of wild ancestors. Among the believers in reincarnation, however, atavism is not a matter of genes but of transmigration of the personality. Primitive tribes were convinced that the likeness of a child to his parent or grandparent was due to reincarnation. And from time to time, one also hears such reasoning carried to further extremes: Did Napoleon try again to conquer Russia, in the form of Hitler? Was Stalin really the reincarnation of the despotic Roman emperor Caligula? If some of the startling resemblances between persons who lived centuries apart are not examples of reincarnation, they might just be Mother Nature's way. Either she didn't want to go on creating different types indefinitely, or else she ran out of ideas, so she began duplicating for the benefit of mankind.

Whatever the answer, the fact is that reincarnation has been given some serious thought. Today, science also is dealing with a wide range of related subjects such as spiritualism (the idea that mediums or others can communicate with the dead), mental telepathy (thought transference and mind reading), clairvoyance (awareness of objects and events not normally perceptible), precognition (the ability to predict events) and psychokinesis (the influencing of physical events through the mind).

One of the earliest known American cases of apparent reincarnation to interest scientists involved a little girl named Nellie Foster. In the 1890's, her father had lost another daughter, Maria. The family moved from Illinois to the Dakotas, where Nellie was born. While there, Nellie insisted on referring to herself as Maria, saying that her father always used to call her that. Later, her father took her on a business trip to the town in Illinois where the family had lived. Amazingly, Nellie recognized the family's former home and a number of neighbors she had never met but who knew her late sister, and not only identified the school Maria had attended, but Maria's desk as well, announcing, "That desk is mine."

Then, in the 1900's, there were the celebrated investigations of one Colonel Rochas, a retired French Army engineer who dabbled in psychology in an attempt to prove that souls transmigrate. By hypnosis, he claimed to have forced memory to travel backward through previous periods of the soul's life. One young woman the colonel hypnotized was able to recall previous existences as a peasant during the time of Napoleon, a soldier under Louis XV and an old woman of an earlier date. About thirty years old, the woman was put into a hypnotic sleep with the suggestion that she float back to her younger days. After a while, Rochas asked her: "How old are you, mademoiselle?"

"Just turning twenty," she replied, giving her maiden name, the names of her friends when she was that age and recounting her daily activities. (These were investigated later and found to be correct.)

Then Rochas suggested she was a teen-ager. The subject changed her voice to that of a younger girl and discussed that period of her life. Rochas told her she was but a child, clinging to her mother's skirts. This time the sleeping woman lapsed into baby talk and started to coo. Rochas next told her that she was to go still farther backward, and the woman's words changed into unclear sounds. Rochas continued to question his subject. Suddenly, the woman spoke again, but this time her voice was deep, gruff and unmistakably that of a man. She said she was Jean Bourdon, a peasant, and that his two sons were fighting with Napoleon in Russia. Rochas asked Jean to go back farther and the subject began to talk about the French Revolution, noting that he had witnessed the execution of Louis XVI and later ran behind the tumbril that bore Marie Antoinette to the scaffold. Under more questioning, Jean said he had been a soldier under Louis XV and had stood guard at Versailles at the apartment of Comtesse du Barry, Louis's mistress. Rochas then suggested to Jean that he was about to die, and the hypnotized subject responded by speaking in the voice of an old woman. She said her name was Madelaine and that she was a lacemaker.

Rochas was about to proceed when a physician ordered the demonstration stopped in consideration of the subject's health. Later, it was determined that a man named Jean Bourdon had lived, until 1812, in the native village of the hypnotized woman. Church records there also established the existence of a Madelaine Carterot during the period of Louis XV. Rochas concluded: "I consider that the test proves my contention. The present incarnation took place in 1870, when the soul of the man who died in 1812 took possession of her body, doubtless after dwelling in another body during the interim. Jean Bourdon's soul had a previous incarnation in the person of Madelaine Carterot. Could I but keep a subject under hypnotic spell for a day or a week, I could go much further into the past. Perhaps, we might learn the whole history of mankind."

Rochas's investigations had a modern-day parallel in the case of Bridey Murphy. In 1956, a Colorado businessman with hypnotism for a hobby, Morey Bernstein, led a hypnotized housewife back through the years to the age of one. He suggested that she go back in memory and, according to his account, she did — to a time before her birth when she was Bridey Murphy, an Irish girl of the nineteenth century. The story, told in a best-selling book and a movie, was hailed by those who felt it proved the theory of reincarnation and debunked by others who felt it proved nothing but the existence of a fertile imagination.

Recently, in a more scientific vein, the head of a unit in India studying parapsychology (a term used for extrasensory perception, telepathy and clairvoyance) presented findings of a study on how the earlier personality determines the personality of the reincarnation. Dr. Jamuna Prasad, according to a report in the British journal *Nature*, believed he found that reborn children between the ages of two and five show strong memories of their previous life. When these memories sharply disagree with their present way of life, conflicts arise. In one case, for example, an apparently reincarnated boy hated the sight of a certain type of cereal because, according to the study, the first incarnation died of overeating out of love for it. In another, an Indian girl who had supposedly lived in England in her previous life could not adjust to her present vegetarian family's diet, preferred meat and missed eating with a knife and fork. Another boy, who had previously been a Brahmin, was reincarnated into a lowly caste and was very unhappy, refusing to eat anything.

There have been thousands of such accounts. Some are difficult to explain, others are not. Often, a person will have the feeling "I have been here before," or "I have done this before," when they know they haven't. This, however, does not necessarily mean he has been reincarnated. Psychologists call such a feeling *déjà vu*. They define this as the *illusion* of having previously experienced something that is actually being experienced for the first time. What it actually may be is a form of defense, for it usually occurs during anxious moments. For instance, when one says, "I have been through this before," he may be telling himself, "and I made it without a scratch, even though I was afraid." Another explanation for cases of apparent reincarnation is that the subject may have forgotten that he was exposed to some event or person that left an impression. Or his subconscious mind might have picked up and hidden away bits and pieces of information from, say, an open history book or a casual conversation nearby while he daydreamed his way through a math assignment in a library. Insofar as the use of hypnotism to bring about age-regression is concerned, hypnotists are able to press their subjects with leading questions often suggestive of the answers expected. Thus, a hypnotized person might not be relating past experiences, but occurrences suggested by the hypnotist, much as a fiction writer weaves a tale around some minor incident. It has also been demonstrated that virtually all kinds of dreams can be produced when a subject is in a deep hypnotic sleep.

The reincarnation theory has been assailed by Christian theologians who teach that each human soul is created by God at the time of its infusion into the human body and does not preexist. They see it as directly opposed to Scripture, specifically the words of St. Paul to the Hebrews, "It is appointed unto man to die once, but after this comes the judgment." Reincarnation, theologians maintain, is psychologically unsound because it denies the unity of the human individual and his personality, which is based on the union of the soul and the body.

The beliefs in reincarnation and life after death raise another tantalizing question: Can the living communicate with the dead? Again, the answer depends on whom you ask. Most churchmen and scientists are skeptical, but many people, including churchmen and scientists, believe such a thing is possible. A few years ago when Episcopal Bishop James A. Pike declared he had communicated with his dead son, he was subjected to a barrage of criticism. But to those who encourage the study of psychic phenomena there was nothing wrong with the bishop's assertion. "The Bible," said the Reverend William V. Rauscher, president of an organization devoted to examining such phenomena within the context of religion, "is full of paranormal experience. It's just that people get upset if we say Jesus practiced levitation, instead of simply saying that He walked on water." Even William James, the psychologist-philosopher, affiliated himself with a society for psychical research in the belief that such phenomena should be investigated thoroughly.

The American cult of spiritualism probably was started in 1848 with three sisters—Margaret, Leah and Catherine Fox of Hydeville, New York. The girls claimed to have heard mysterious rappings in their home, and suggested that the spirits of the dead communicated with the living in this way. The spirits supposedly rapped once for no, twice for doubtful and three times for yes. Using that code, along with a more complicated one for spelling out messages, they quickly made the Fox home a center of attraction and controversy. Despite allegations that the spirit knocks were produced by trickery, spiritualism caught on, and a number of mediums, some sincere, some outright frauds, came along.

Among the outstanding thinkers who believed in spirit communication were Arthur Conan Doyle, Sherlock Holmes's creator, and Sir Oliver Lodge, an English physicist and writer who died in 1940. Lodge, whose scientific work included studies of electromagnetic waves and lightning, was convinced that human survival beyond the grave could be scientifically proved. "I make this assertion," he said, "on definite scientific grounds. I know that certain departed friends of mine still exist because I have talked with them as I could converse through a telephone with someone at a distance. Being men of cultivated mind, they have given proofs that it is really they, not some impersonation, not something emanating from myself. I tell you with all the strength of conviction that I can muster, that they do persist, that they take an interest in what is going on here, and that they help us." Among the dead people Lodge claimed to have communicated with was his son, Raymond, who was killed on a Flanders battlefield in World War I. When Lodge died he left secret messages, unseen by any other living person, sealed in an envelope, and promised he would repeat them "from the other side." Thus far, Lodge hasn't been heard from.

Spiritualism got one of its biggest boosts when Sir William Crookes (1832–1919), an eminent English chemist and physicist and discoverer of the element thallium, announced that he believed in ghosts. He set out to prove that there was something to spiritualism with the same cool calculation that was the hallmark of his usual scientific work. Crookes spent a good deal of his time examining the phenomena produced at séances by a remarkable man, a Scotch immigrant named Daniel Dunglas Home. Home, who conducted all his séances in bright light, is considered one of the most important figures in spiritualism, and much of what he did has never been completely explained. Among his feats was one in which he appeared to be raised bodily and propelled through the air; other times he materialized spirit hands and, later, entire spirit forms. In one of Sir William's tests of Home's feats, an accordion was suspended in a cage made of wire. The wires of this "spirit cage," as it was called, were connected to powerful batteries so that anyone trying to manipulate the mechanism would receive a strong shock. Home was called upon to produce a spirit. Sir William described what happened next: "Very soon, the accordion began waving about in a somewhat curious manner. Then sounds came from it, and finally several notes were played in succession. The accordion was expanding and contracting. It began to move about, oscillating around and around the cage and playing at the same time. I and two of the others present saw the accordion distinctly floating about inside the cage with no visible support." Another time, while Sir William was sitting at a séance in his dining room, a hand rose up from an opening in the table and gave him a tiny flower. "On another occasion," he recalled, "a small hand and arm like a baby's appeared to play about a lady who was sitting next to me and patted my arm and pulled my coat several times."

Some people, although convinced that many of the "supernatural" incidents that occurred were genuine, did not believe they were proof of the existence of spirits who communicated from the great beyond. The famous magician Houdini often exposed mediums as frauds by producing the same results with natural, nonmystical trickery. Before his death, Houdini said he would test the powers of mediums with a ten-word code which he would try to send to his wife within ten years of his death. Several mediums claimed they had made contact with him, but none was able to transmit the code to Houdini's wife.

And so it has gone ever since man first appeared on the scene. Immortality has been rejected by those who feel its only basis is wishful thinking — that when the body dies, the personality dies with it because it is part of the physical body. Believers can cite the resurrection of Jesus, and maintain that since life on earth is not completely fulfilled an afterlife is necessary for completion; they believe that since the just often are not rewarded and the unjust often not punished on earth, there has to be a final judgment for the soul. Another argument in favor of an afterlife is that since matter and energy may be transformed but not destroyed, neither can personality, which exists just as do the elements in nature, be destroyed. Still others hold that since immortality has been believed in for so long and by so many people it must be right. And there is the argument that because the spirit appears to be cut loose from our bodies during dreams, it could live a life apart from the body after death, the deepest sleep of all.

Modern philosophers have differed widely on the subject. Baruch Spinoza (1632–1677), for one, believed in an impersonal kind of immortality, one in which personal memory did not survive. "The human mind," wrote this greatest modern expounder of pantheism, "cannot be absolutely destroyed with the human body, but there is some part of it which remains eternal." But, he felt, the mind cannot imagine nor recollect anything except while it is in the body. Jean Jacques Rousseau (1712–1778), an eminent Swiss-French thinker who changed his own religion frequently, said that although reason showed there could be no immortality, man's feelings about the matter were strongly in favor. Because of this, he suggested trusting to instinct rather than yielding to skepticism. For Arthur Schopenhauer (1788–1860), a German philosopher deeply influenced by Buddhist thought, Buddhism was more profound than Christianity because it proposed Nirvana as the supreme goal. Kant felt that a belief in God and immortality was not logical but was based on personal moral feeling. He cautioned against saying, "*It* is morally certain there is a future life." Instead, man should say, "*I* am morally certain there is a future life." William James, with his open mind, saw something in all religions and beliefs, and was himself convinced that there was another world. He put it this way: "I firmly disbelieve, myself, that our human experience is the highest form of experience existent in the universe. I believe, rather, that we stand in much the same relation to the whole of the universe as our canine and feline pets do to the whole of human life. They inhabit our drawing rooms and libraries. They take part in scenes of whose significance they have no inkling. They are merely tangent to curves of history, the beginnings and ends and forms of which pass wholly beyond their ken. So we are tangent to the wider life of things."

The great skeptic of the lot was David Hume (1711–1776), a Scotsman who even denied that there was such a thing as the individual self. Man, he said, had no constant understanding of himself as an entity, and was nothing but a "bundle or collection" or different perceptions. Man, then, could not have any knowledge of facts, and did not perceive the mind because it had no substance, but only had ideas, feelings and memories, which were the mind. He rejected the principle of immortality, and declared that there was no observable soul behind the thought process. For George Santayana (1863–1952), a Spanish-born American skeptic who took a materialistic view of nature, the very fact that man was born was a bad indication for immortality. Rather, he believed: "He who lives in the ideal and leaves it expressed in society or in art enjoys a double immortality."

When one reflects on it, man has had much to say about something he really knows little about, is hardpressed to confirm or deny, and will probably never resolve. Maybe there is a life for each of us after death, maybe not. Maybe it is for sale, maybe it is not. What does seem certain, though, is that with or without a personal existence beyond, life itself will continue to spring up anew in all kinds of forms and shapes, in our children or in the children of others, on this world or on some other world. That which we call the spirit of man will go on creating, reasoning, seeking new truths, changing the face of the earth. Some of it will be for better, some for worse. But either way, this creative spirit, this life, goes relentlessly on, hopefully toward some overall good and noble purpose. And given what we know of life on this planet alone, one cannot reasonably expect that it will suddenly quit, never to appear again. The joke, in the last analysis, is on death. For the victory of the grave is a hollow one that does not turn any tide nor repel any invader. Life is the true victor, for it is a progress and not an end, and in that is immortality.